COMPLETE Snooker

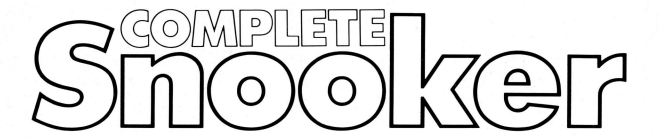

Complete Snooker

Terry Griffiths

With

Julian Worthington

Pelham Books

First published in Great Britain by
Pelham Books Limited
44 Bedford Square
London WC1B 3DU
1984

Acknowledgements Special
photography by Clive Burling.
Photographs were also kindly supplied
by All-Sport, BBC Hulton Picture
Library, David Muscroft, Ifor Jacobs,
Mary Evans Picture Library and
Sporting Pictures. Special thanks to
Mr Barry Hearn for allowing us to
photograph in the Matchroom,
Romford, Essex.

British Library Cataloguing in Publication Data
Griffiths, Terry
    Complete Snooker
    1. Snooker
    I. Title
    794. 7'35   GV900.S

ISBN 0 7207 1502 4

Designed and produced by Editorial Design Consultants Limited,
4 Wedgwood Mews, Greek Street, London W1V 6JN, in association
with Michael Balfour Ltd.
Typesetting by Dorchester Typesetting Group Limited, Dorchester, Dorset.
Reproduction by Precise Litho Limited, 32 Great Sutton Street, London EC1.
and Lithospeed (Sales) Ltd. 32 Paul Street, London EC2.
Printed by Raithby, Lawrence & Company Ltd, Leicester and London.
D.L.B. 42270–1983

Contents

Introduction

I have felt for some time there was a need for a coaching manual that not only covered the techniques of snooker but also looked at the more general aspects of the approach to the game and how to get the most out of it. I have broken up the techniques of snooker into sections, so that you can analyse your own game stage by stage when things go wrong and you are not playing as well as you should.

Naturally it is important for anyone aspiring to play snooker well to master the basic techniques. But I believe this is only part of the challenge. Technique alone will never guarantee success. There is a lot more that goes into making the complete player.

I was fortunate as a youngster to have taken to the game naturally and consequently I never had to work that hard at it. My natural ability served me well as an amateur. But since turning professional in 1978 I have realised just how much of snooker relies on the individual attitude and temperament and not just the skill.

To be honest, as an amateur I had never really stopped to think about my technique or to analyse the good or bad points of my play. It was not until I got involved in coaching others that I became aware of the many difficulties faced by those who did not have this natural ability but had to work to become reasonable players. And it was only then that it struck me how much quicker I would have realised my own potential had I given more thought to the game when I was much younger.

I found coaching was a great experience and there is no doubt that it has given me a real insight into the game and into the people who play it. Do not misunderstand me. I have always given a great deal of thought to the game and my whole approach to snooker has been based on a more general philosophy of life. But only by studying the attitudes and approach of others was I able to put my beliefs into a wider perspective and to understand how best to give advice to those wanting to learn.

Ideally I should have liked to have been here coaching you all in person. However, I hope this book will prove valuable to all who read it – whether you are picking up a cue for the first time or have been playing for years but are looking to improve on the weaker aspects of your game. Or perhaps you are one of the millions who play the game, but have never stopped to analyse how you play and

Coaching has given me a far greater insight into the game and helped me to understand the problems that players without a natural ability run into on the snooker table.

where you could be going wrong.

The first point I hope to bring across in *Complete Snooker* is that you should always aim to make the game as simple as possible. Snooker is a difficult enough game to master and play well, as it is. The last thing you want to do is make it any harder for yourself. That is why, for example, I have not laid too much emphasis on such things as side spin or combination shots. They are, in any case, a very small part of the game in terms of the number of times you may feel the need to use them. And, more often than not, there is another shot available to you that is simpler and therefore has more chance of being successful.

That is not to say that you should restrict yourself to a limited number of shots you know you can play. I am a great believer in having as wide a range of shots available as possible, since you never know when you may have to use them. You may well be reasonably successful even if you deliberately avoid playing certain shots, but you will never become a complete player.

When I say you should keep the game simple, what I mean is that you should not necessarily go for the harder shot, when the easier one will do you just as well. Sometimes there is no choice. But when there is, take it.

Of course the same applies with your basic technique. The simpler it is, the more chance it has of being right every time. The aim of all players is to perfect a technique that suits them and their style of play to the extent that they do it automatically. Because, when each shot is played, you must have your mind concentrated 100 per cent on that particular shot. You do not therefore want to be worrying about a certain aspect of your stance, for example, or your cue action. And the simpler all of these things are, the less of a problem or worry they are likely to be.

This is one of the main reasons why I believe any technique book should be treated more as a guide than a gospel. As long as you have understood the principles behind the technique and appreciate what the right effect should be and how errors in technique can affect your play, then you should be able to work at your own – and not necessarily copy others religiously.

Of course, you must study carefully the advice given. Technique has been developed by individual players over many years and their experience and knowledge has got to be worth a lot. Look closely at how other people play, try out the slight variations in technique and see which ones suit you and help your game. I believe this flexibility is vital if you are to build up a style of play that suits you.

I can only tell you in *Complete Snooker* how I have developed my technique over the years to reach the standard I have. As I explain, I have tried different things – some of which have worked, others of which I have given up. This is an important process, whatever standard you have reached. You should never be frightened to experiment or look to improve your game, even if you feel happy with the way it is.

I believe the key to playing well is balance. In all aspects of the game – basic technique, matchplay, practice and temperament – balance is the overriding factor.

When you start to learn snooker – or any sport for that matter – everything is balanced against you. As you begin to grasp the basic techniques and manage to cope with the elementary aspects, the balance starts to move in your favour until you reach a point where technique becomes automatic and you can concentrate on the game as a whole.

It is like learning to drive. When you first get into a car, you have to master the controls and get the car moving safely along the road before you can think about the finer points that will hopefully make you a good driver.

You will see in *Complete Snooker* how much emphasis I put on getting the basics right first. Once you are in control of the stance, the cue grip and the cue action, then you can move on to the harder things such as hitting the white ball correctly. I cannot stress enough how difficult it is just to stand in the right position, without even moving the cue. If, within three months, you can stand correctly and guarantee to hit the white ball in the centre, you are a genius.

So the balance comes into technique, learning stage by stage to gain complete control of the basics, until you can stop thinking about this part of the game and start concentrating on the more difficult aspects, such as hitting the white and potting balls. Balance is also important in matchplay. You need to strike a balance between attack and defence. You also have to be able to weigh up the various options you have on a shot, depending on the position of the balls on the table and the situation in the match itself.

You need to strike a balance when it comes to practising. How often and how long should you practise? When should you take a break and when do you need to relax and do something else? There is no point in practising for hours on end before a match and work yourself up to a peak, only to find when you get onto the match table you cannot pot a ball.

The final balance, which is relevant to the others, is in yourself. In practice, you can be the best player in the club. Everything you do on the table goes right. But when it comes to competitions, your game goes to pieces. So temperament is really the key to success – and this is where a lot of good players fall down. On the night, they just have not got what it takes to cope with the pressures of matchplay.

This mental balance is the hardest of all to attain – and many players never achieve it. And it is reflected not just at the snooker table or on the playing field, but in your whole lifestyle. You must be able to switch off and cut out everything except what is in front of you, whether it is playing for a difficult pot or getting out of a snooker. You must be able to put that last shot behind you, even if you missed it by a mile. You must be able to ignore the fact that your opponent has just made a large break and take the opportunity to get back on the table. The person who can maintain this mental balance, despite problems and disappointments, is the one who may lose a few battles but will eventually win the war.

Tied in with this idea of balance is control, which is why I have divided up the techniques of the game into four sections – body control, cue control, cue ball control and self-control. I believe you will only become the complete player if you can master these four controls. If you can master two of them, you are doing very well!

The first stage of learning the game involves controlling the position of your body – getting the stance right with the feet in position, holding the cue correctly, bridging and sighting down the line of the shot. Having mastered what I regard as the basic techniques, you then have to work at controlling the cue. This involves the complete cue action – feathering, pausing, hitting, following through and stopping – and how to pot balls, whether in a straight line or at an angle to the pocket.

When you have learned how to bring the cue through correctly to hit the white ball in the right place and pot the object ball, you can then go on to the next control – that of the cue ball. This is, of course, important for break-building, since you must be able to put the white ball where you want on the table for your next shot. This section includes the techniques of applying spin and playing with power.

The final control – that of yourself – is the hardest of them all. Yet without it you are unlikely to master the others.

I have included in these sections different ways of practising the controls – learning to hit the white ball straight and how to work out angles. The advice I have given is not just for the beginner. There are always times when aspects of your game go wrong or suddenly prove to be a problem. When this happens, you can – and must – go back to the basics. Check on the four controls and see where you are going wrong. It may be that just one control is to blame – or more, possibly.

In my experience the person who plays the game day in and day out rarely, if ever, gives any thought to why his game is fluctuating. But it is as important for him as it is for the beginner to check on the basics. Only by analysing your game and working out where you are going wrong will you ever make real progress in snooker.

I find that personal experiences can be helpful in explaining what can happen and what needs to be done to put things right. Everyone goes through difficult patches at times. I have and so have all the top players. The way I solved the problems is obviously not the only way. All I can say is that it worked for me and may work for you too.

That, in essence, is how I want you to approach *Complete Snooker*. There are plenty of books telling you this way is right or that way is right. What I have aimed to do in my book is to help you choose the right way for you, whether you are picking up the cue for the first time or want to find out where you are going wrong or how to improve your present standard.

At the end of the day, it is the person who has the controls and maintains the right balance and plays consistently well who will be successful. Your task is to study that person, look at the techniques used and try them out. Some may be helpful, others may not. But unless you experiment, you will never find out. And without a reasonable level of ability, you will never enjoy the game of snooker – which, for me, is what it is all about.

History of the game

John Roberts, Junr.

Chapter: 1
History of the game

Of all the millions of people who either play or watch the game of snooker, I wonder how many know when and where the game started and how it developed to the sport we have today. Snooker itself dates back to 1875, but we have to turn the clock back much further than that to find the first recognisable form of this table game — billiards,

Louis XIV playing Single Pool at Versailles. On the table you can see the 'king' and the 'port'.

around which the modern game of snooker was based.

Although the exact origins are uncertain, the first known form of billiards has been attributed to a 16th century French artist called Henrique Devigne. There is evidence of a type of billiard table even earlier than this — in the 1460s. By the mid-17th century the game was much in fashion in France, thanks to the attentions of Louis XIV. It was mentioned in Spenser's *Mother Hubbard's Tale* (1591) and by Shakespeare in *Antony and Cleopatra* (c. 1607).

The scene at St James's Hall, London, in February 1870 during the first official title match for the British Billiards championship. The result was victory for William Cook over John Roberts Senior.

Above: The draw in March 1933 for the English Billiards Professional championship held at the Billiards Association and Control Council offices in The Strand, London. With the two officials on the right are (from left) Clark McConachy, Joe Davis, Tom Newman and (far right) Walter Lindrum.

Far left: Edwin Kentfield, the 'first' champion around 1820, demonstrates the stance.

Left: John Roberts Junior, who avenged his father's title match defeat by beating William Cook two months later – in April 1870.

Above: Looking more like characters out of an American gangster film than billiards players, Joe Davis (second right) and Tom Newman (far right) arrive at Burroughes for the start of the 1924 season.
Right: William Cook on his way to victory against John Roberts Senior in February 1870.

*Above: Walter Lindrum
(left) and Joe Davis striking
for the break before their
match at the New Holborn
Billiard Hall, London, in
1930.
Right: Standing
uncomfortably close to the
table, Tom Newman
watches a shot by Joe
Davis during their match at
the start of the 1924
billiards season.*

In England, the earliest description of the game appeared in Cotton's *Compleat Gamester* (1674) and was played on a table, the bed of which was made of oak and occasionally marble. Slate beds were introduced in about 1827. The cushions were originally stuffed with flock, but by 1835 rubber ones were being made. Pockets, originally called hazards, were simply wooden boxes, later to be replaced by nets. And the early players pushed the balls with a mace made of heavy wood and tipped at the broad end with ivory.

At one time the game itself was known as Single Pool. The principle was that you won a life if you potted an opponent's ball and lost a life if you potted your own. A small ivory arch known as a 'port' and an ivory peg or 'king' stood on the table and you could also score by passing the 'port' or touching the 'king'.

By 1734 these additions to the table had been abandoned. Maces were still used, but by now cues were also allowed. Until the early 19th century these had no tips. Credit for these is due to an imprisoned French soldier named Mingaud who, during his many hours of enforced practice, developed a leather tip and was able to demonstrate the advantages in cuemanship that this additional piece of equipment afforded.

Around 1775 people were playing a game known as carambole. This involved using a third ball on the table and this ball was called the carom. The striker scored with winning hazards (pots) and caroms (cannons) — and so the game of billiards as we would recognise it today was established.

Edwin Kentfield was regarded as the first champion of British billiards — as far back as 1820. But the title was not played for until February 1870 when William Cook beat John Roberts Senior. Roberts' son, also John, was to avenge that defeat just two months later. The first official set of rules was drawn up with the formation of the Billiards Association in 1885. This body was made up of amateurs and professionals. In 1908 the rival Billiards Control Club was set up and there were then two lots of rules until the two amalgamated in 1919 — to be known as the Billiards Association and Control Council.

The main architects of the modern game of billiards were Edwin Kentfield and John Roberts Junior. Kentfield was instrumental in the development and improvement of the equipment — tables, cushions and cues. Roberts in his turn developed a whole range of new techniques of play and could be said to have founded the modern professional game of billiards.

By this time, snooker had been invented, although like billiards there is some doubt as to its exact origins. One theory is that the game originated at the Royal Military Academy in Woolwich. Here, first-year cadets were called 'snookers' — a corruption of the French word 'neux' meaning a newly joined cadet. This theory is obviously connected with the most popularly accepted origin of the game — at Jubbulpore in India in 1875 by a young subaltern in the Devonshire Regiment — Neville Chamberlain.

Apparently Chamberlain had suggested adding coloured balls onto the table to vary the popular 'Black Pool' that was then being played. According to the story, one of the players was called a 'regular snooker' when he failed to pot an easy colour. The association here was with the failure of a first-year cadet — that is a 'snooker' — back at Woolwich.

In an attempt to relieve the injured party, Chamberlain suggested that they were all 'snookers' at the game — and that this would be an appropriate name for it. Snooker finally reached England in 1885, after John Roberts had toured India and brought back the rules.

The game then made great strides, although it was not until the early 1930s that it began to rival billiards in popularity — in terms of the numbers playing and watching. By the late 1930s, however, it had overtaken billiards.

The history of professional snooker has really been the history of the Davis brothers — Joe and Fred. Joe, the great master and originator of modern technique, was undefeated in all 15 world championships from the start of the competition in 1927 until 1946. Fred reached every final from 1947 until 1956 and during that time took eight titles. In the second half of the 1960s (there were no world professional championships from 1958 until 1964), John Pulman successfully defended the title he had won in 1957 against a succession of single challengers. The player of the 1970s, without doubt, was Ray Reardon. Between 1970 and 1978 he won the world title six times — before surrendering it to me in 1979!

Equipment

Chapter: 2
Equipment

Equipment obviously plays an important part in the game of snooker. The degree to which it will affect your own game will depend on quality and conditions. In some cases – such as with the table – there is little you as a player can do except adapt your play to suit the conditions and state of the table at the time. The quality and condition of the cue and tip are, however, very much down to the player and must be your responsibility.

The table

It is a common mistake to believe that all tables are the same. The more you play, the more you will realise how much tables can vary and the enormous differences in playing conditions. The standard full-size table is 12ft × 6ft and there is now a wide range of smaller sizes, the quality of which is improving all the time. But even though these tables may look the same, they will all have their own characteristics. And you will only discover these by playing on them regularly.

So what should you be looking for on a table? To start with, the cloth should have a good nap on it. The chances are you will not be playing on a new cloth, but there should not be undue wear on it. The more worn the cloth, the harder it is for spins to take effect without a great deal of effort from the player.

The pockets should be of a reasonable size – and this does not mean that they are actually larger. When people talk about big pockets, what they are refering to is the amount of undercut in the rubber on the cushion round the edge of the pockets. If you go back to the days of Joe Davis, the pockets were regarded as small, since there was hardly any undercut on them. Recently, the trend has been the other way – with much more undercut round the pockets.

What, then, is a reasonable size of pocket? As far as I am concerned, if you hit a ball correctly along, for example, the bottom cushion – however hard – the pocket should take it in. Unfortunately there are not many tables about on which you can do this and it does restrict the more skilful players.

The quality of the cushions is also important and here there should be a balance with the nap of the cloth. What I mean here is that there should be a balance between the speed at which the ball comes off the cushion and the speed at which it runs over the cloth. It is no good if the ball comes off the cushion quickly and then slows down on the cloth – or equally, comes slowly off the cushion and then carries on running across the table.

As I said earlier, unless you have your own table there is little you can do about the condition except to be aware of it and try to adjust your game accordingly to suit. You must understand that tables can differ from day to day with the change in atmosphere, even though they have been brushed and ironed correctly.

To explain what I mean, try to consider conditions in a major championship tournament. There may be 1000 people in the hall during the afternoon session and 2000 by the evening session. For a start, twice as much body heat is generated and there will be more dampness in the cloth. You can see this when you put your hand down and then lift it off, since it will leave a hand-print on the cloth.

Obviously the average player will not meet with such extreme conditions, but it is important to realise that dampness in the cloth will effect the pace of the balls and the effect of spin. After all, you only have to look at cricket or bowls, for example, to see the difference damp conditions will make to the behaviour of the ball. Because snooker is an indoor game, people tend to assume that the table will not be affected by atmospheric conditions. But it can be.

I am not an expert on cloths. But the wool used is brushed and ironed one way and the nap of the cloth therefore goes in one direction. So in theory you should have the ball breaking in certain places – or falling off as we call it – with the nap. Unfortunately it does not quite work like that. You can play on one table where the ball breaks as expected, then go to another where the nap is thinner or, perhaps, the iron was too hot and the ball does not break as expected and you miss the pot.

I am afraid you will only recognise the varying conditions of tables through experience. As a beginner, the tables will almost certainly look the same. You will not notice that the cloth is dark green or light green, that there is either a lot of nap which will make spins that much easier to effect or that there is little nap and the cloth is shiny, making control that much harder.

Even in local clubs, conditions have improved dramatically over the last few years and tables are of a much higher standard and better cared for. Since the whole game of snooker is about control of the white ball, you will never play well on a sub-standard table. Of course, there is not much you can do about this, as I have said. But it is important to understand what makes a good table and to be able to recognise the good and bad points of a particular table before you start playing on it.

Although the quality of the table and the way it plays will vary enormously, the position of the baulk line and the 'D' is always the same. Here the two are being clearly marked before the start of a championship match.

I am often asked whether it is all right to play on a small table. The fact is that it is better to play on the floor than not to hit a ball at all. Obviously the ideal situation is to play on a full-size table. But small tables can be invaluable when you are starting to learn the game as a youngster. This is the type I began on – and it was the same with Steve Davis. As long as you have a cue in your hand and you are trying to hit the ball, this has got to be progress.

The basic point to remember, which I shall be discussing later when we get to potting technique, is that for every shot you are aiming to hit the white ball in a straight line – and this principle is the same whether you are on a 4ft, 6ft or 12ft table. And, in fact, the playing angles are more or less the same on the smaller tables.

The small table is an ideal way of bringing young people into the game. If they start enjoying playing on that and have some success because the pockets are easier and closer, they may go on from there. They will soon realise that a full-size table offers a much greater challenge, but by then they have got the bug and will want to keep on playing. At one time you had a job to get a good quality small table because there was not a big enough market.

Now the market is enormous – and the standard and range greatly increased. This development really has brought snooker into every home.

The balls

I firmly believe that the great advances made in technique in recent years are in no small part due to the changes in the manufacture of the balls. The ones used in all major tournaments – and now in many clubs too – are known as Super Crystalate balls. The playing angles are slightly different and it is much easier to impart spin on the ball, making control of the white ball that much easier too.

It is worth mentioning the fact that if I find myself playing with older type balls – such as the Crystalate – everything is different and I have to adjust my timing and mechanism for each shot. I have at times miscued before getting the feel right. This shows what a difference the balls can have on your game, depending on the type you are used to.

With advances in technology, we have come a long way since the early days of billiards, when wooden balls were used, and even the days of Joe Davis, when snooker was played with ivory balls.

The cue

I play with a very thin, unorthodox type of cue which, I am told, is probably 80 or so years old. It weighs about 14oz, whereas the standard cue today would be about 16½oz, with a 10mm tip. Basically it is important to get a cue that looks right and feels right. Do you like the colour and the grain of wood – or maybe the name of the professional on it – and what does it feel like when you pick it up?

The majority of cues are made with either ash or maple. Ash has a stronger grain, which some people prefer and use to ensure they are holding the cue in the same position for each shot. Steve Davis does this. Personally I do not like a strong grain and use a maple cue, where it is less obvious. But, there again, I do not necessarily play with the cue held in exactly the same position each time.

The standard length for a cue is 4ft 10in. I do not agree with one popularly held belief that the shorter you are the shorter your cue should be, since it could well restrict your cue action, which I shall be talking about later. I think you should play with one of standard length and hold it a bit higher up the butt if necessary. If you find after playing for a while that the cue is too long, you can always trim a bit off, although I would not recommend this.

Some people like to feel a thick butt in their hand, while

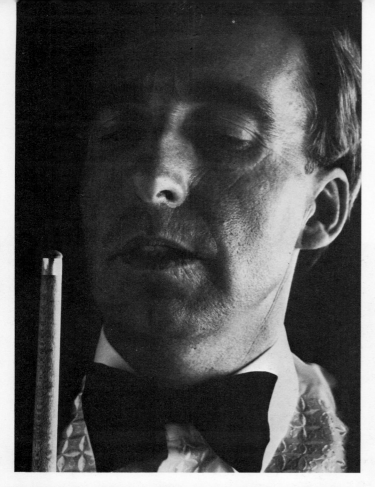

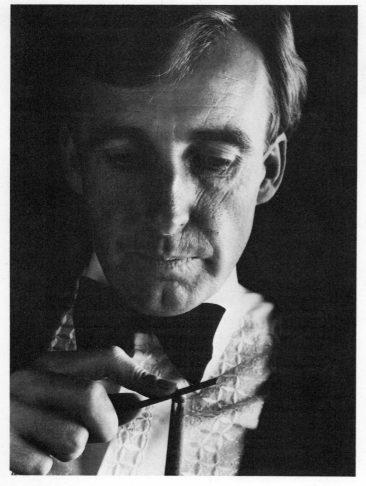

Left: The tip is a vitally important part of the cue since it is this that makes contact with the white ball. Always replace it before it shows signs of excessive wear and make sure it is properly trimmed flush with the ferrule or it will affect your sighting.

Below left: Use a small file to give the tip a domed shape and roughen up the surface slightly when it wears smooth. Be careful not to damage the ferrule or tear off the tip as you do this.

others prefer a slimmer one. Again, some players like a thicker shaft on the cue. At the end of the day it is really a matter of personal preference.

Of course the cue must be straight. And the way to check this is not — as I did for years, I must admit — roll it on the table. Most people do this, but you should look down the cue and see if it has any bends. If you roll it on the table, it could have two bends off-setting each other, in which case it will still roll straight.

I play with a one-piece cue, as do the majority of professionals. But this is because we have had our cues for years and do not want to change them. It takes a long time to get used to a new cue and most people will resist the change.

If I was taking up the game tomorrow I would definitely use a two-piece cue. Everyone will tell you the same. For a number of reasons this type is a lot more practical. It is much more convenient to carry about since its case is much smaller. Another value for those who take the game more seriously is the fact that you can have two identical top sections and break in two tips at once. This way, if one tip wears down too much or comes off, you have a replacement on hand to use straight away. This could be very important if, as a competition player, you have reached a critical stage in the season. And if for any reason one part of the cue is damaged, you need only buy a replacement section — and not the whole cue.

One other advantage of a two-piece cue, incidentally, is that it will not warp as quickly or easily as a one-piece cue. Proper care of the cue should prevent this happening anyway, but not everyone looks after the cue properly.

When this type of cue was first produced, there was concern about the joint and whether it would hold out. But the manufacturers have now perfected this part.

The tip

People tend to forget how important the tip is, but it is the only part of the cue that is in contact with the white ball — for every shot you play. For this reason, I believe everyone should put their own tip on the cue. If you make a point of doing this — and it is only a ten-minute job — you will know it is on correctly and take care of it.

Make sure the tip is fitted flush with the ferrule and edge of the cue. If the tip is hanging over, this is bound to affect your sighting, since — as I will explain later — you should be using the tip of the cue when you sight up for shots.

When you fit the tip, make sure both contact surfaces —

The table must be brushed and ironed regularly — and always with the nap of the cloth. If the iron is too hot, however, it will flatten the nap and this will affect the control you want over the balls, which I talk about later in the book.

the bottom of the tip and the end of the cue — are perfectly smooth, level and clean. You can use sandpaper or a file for this, but make sure you do not damage the ferrule or touch the top of the tip, since it may leave bits on your striking surface. If you are replacing a tip, make sure you have cleaned away all the old adhesive.

Spread contact adhesive lightly on both fixing surfaces, leave them for 10 minutes and then stick the tip on. If you rush the job and do not ensure the surfaces are smooth and clean, the tip will come off. It should not come off if the job is done properly. The tip should be slightly domed and you can shape it carefully with a small file. Again make sure you do not damage the ferrule.

The amount and type of wear on the tip depends on the player. My tip does tend to wear down slightly more on one side because I do tend to hold it in a particular place for certain shots. But it does not wear down as quickly in one place as Steve Davis's. He always holds his cue in the same position.

The chalk

Chalk is used to improve the grip of the tip on the white ball. The secret is to chalk lightly and regularly. You do not want to cake the tip — equally you should not play with a shiny tip. Green chalk is the most popular, since it does not seem so noticeable when it comes off on the white ball. Blue

shows up more. Cheaper chalks are much harder and you will soon notice this because the chalk will not come off onto the tip as easily. Avoid using them.

Care of the cue

As with a cricketer's bat, a tennis player's racquet or a golfer's clubs, you must look after your cue at all times. You must have a case to keep it in and you should put the cue in it whenever you are not playing. Never leave the cue lying about on the table or lean it up against a wall. If you do put it down for a minute or two, lay it flat. You can, of course, lean the case up.

Each time I play, I wipe my cue with a damp cloth. You would be surprised at the amount of dirt that comes off. I am told that keeping a certain amount of moisture in the cue extends its life. And wash your hands before you play to ensure your grip is right and that dirt is not transferred onto the table or does not affect the cueing action through the bridge hand.

It is not until you reach a certain standard in the game, where you are reliant on the cue you know and are used to, that you will appreciate how precious it is. The problems of breaking or losing your cue can be enormous — as I remember from my amateur days and as Ray Reardon will tell you from his experience a few years ago. So you must look after it at all times.

Body control

Chapter: 3
Body control

This is the first of the four controls I regard as the key to becoming a complete snooker player and is about controlling the position of your body and the cue in your hand. The techniques involved in this type of control I consider as absolutely basic and vital if you have any serious intention of trying to master the game.

It is therefore essential that you master these techniques and can claim to have complete control over your body before you even consider getting down to the table to hit a ball.

Taking up position

Once a player gets to the snooker table, there is a great tendency to rush in and hit the balls without stopping to think properly about their position on the table and therefore the type of shot that should be played. So the approach to the table is dictated by the position of the balls.

What many people do not realise is that you must take sight of the shot you want to play before you get down — even before you put your legs in position. You often see beginners shuffling around and adjusting their position once they are down. More experienced players will make sure they choose the correct position before they get down and will not then move until they have played the shot.

So you should now be able to see how important a part of the game the approach to the table is. After years of experience you will probably not even think about it; you will do it automatically because you will have grown so used to lining up a certain stroke at all the different angles. With the break-off, of course, the balls are always in the same position and therefore your approach will be the same each time. At any other time, however, your approach will be determined by where the balls are on the table for each shot you play.

When you approach the table, you are taking up the line of sight, which is why it is so important to get it right. You will not see an experienced player going down and then shuffling his feet or moving his head or arms about. Once he is down he remains quite still until he hits the cue ball — apart, of course, from moving the cue.

Before you get down to the selected position from where you will strike the ball, you should always have clear in your mind what type of shot you are going to play rather than decide when you are down on the stroke. By that stage your mind should be perfectly clear to concentrate on the shot you want to play, be it attacking or defensive, screw

back or run through or whatever. Everything else should already be fixed in your mind.

If, when you get down, you are not happy with your position — or, maybe, you are having second thoughts about the shot you have selected — then you must get up from the table and start again.

Cue grip

Probably the simplest way to describe the cue grip is by saying: Lay the cue on the table and then pick it up in your hand. This basically is the grip. It must be firm, yet relaxed. If you grip it too tightly, you are bound to tense the muscles in the hand and wrist, your arm will stiffen and therefore will not move smoothly through the cue action that follows. Equally the grip must not be too loose since every shot must be played firmly and positively — even the softest of touches on the white ball.

Keep your fingers together, with the thumb resting on the forefinger. Remember it is the front part of the hand — the thumb and first two fingers — that is actually holding the cue. The other two fingers are there to help with the balance and control, to keep the cue in a straight line.

Depending on how near the butt end you hold the cue, the little finger may wrap round the bottom. I don't think this makes any difference to the technique of cue action. Normally my hand grips the cue about an inch away from the end. For some shots, however, it may move to the end of the cue — when, for example, I am playing a power shot and want maximum back swing or when I am bridging at full stretch. Equally, for very soft shots, I may move the grip up the cue slightly to shorten the cue action — when, for example, I am playing for a snooker and want just to roll the white behind a colour.

You can check on the position of the grip by the knuckles, which should be in a line roughly parallel to the floor and in line with the cue.

Stance

I have already stressed the importance of taking up the correct position before you get down onto the table. To start with, your feet must be in the right place and the right distance from the table so that your weight is forward onto your bridge hand. You can check whether the balance is correct by lifting the bridge hand. Your weight should take you forward onto the table.

Your left foot should be pointing in the same direction as the line of the shot, although it does not have to be exactly

in line with the white and object balls. The right foot should be placed behind the left and pointing out at an angle of about 60 degrees, with the heels of the two feet about 14in apart (see diagram). The feet must be solid to the floor and should not, for the average shot, lift at all. Keep the right leg straight, to act as a brace, and bend the left leg at the knee just enough to get the cue as horizontal as possible, although this will be restricted by the height of the cushion.

The angle of the stance does vary from player to player, but you should aim to develop as much of a sideways stance as possible to get the relevant parts of the body in line with the cue. You will see what I mean when we look at the bridge and sighting down the cue.

When you take up the sideways stance, you must make

See how the cue is tucked nicely into the palm of the hand (left), with the grip firm but relaxed and the back arm straight. Looking side-on, note that the knuckles and cue are in a line roughly parallel to the floor.

This side-on view of the complete stance illustrates the key points to remember when you get down to play. The back arm is vertical from the elbow down and the chin just touches the cue to help keep it as horizontal as possible. Note the slight tension in the left arm.

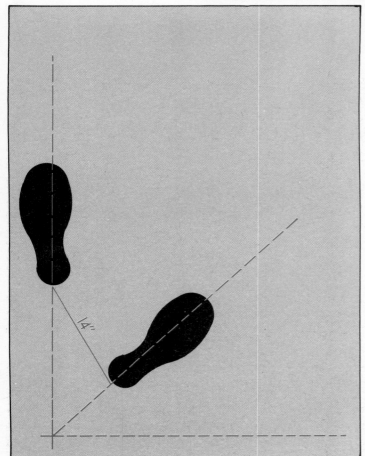

From the plan of the feet you can see that the left one is roughly in line with the shot, while the right points out at approximately 60 degrees. The measurements relate to my stance and naturally yours may vary slightly. But while the distance between the feet will depend on your size, you should maintain the angle of the feet to ensure a solid and balanced position.

sure there is sufficient clearance for your cue and back hand to follow through without the body being in the way.

The bridge

As I have already mentioned, the bridge takes most of the weight forward from the body and through to the pads of the fingers, which should be spread over the cloth. If you are bridging correctly with the right stance, this will feel uncomfortable to begin with. But you must persevere until you get the feel of this position.

It is vital that the bridge remains firm throughout the cue action, since any movement will affect the accuracy of the hit and you are then unlikely to make the contact on the white ball that you intended. Where there is room on the cloth – as with most shots – spread your hand on the table with the pads of the fingers gripping the cloth and the thumb cocked to provide a deep 'V' through which the cue moves. Fortunately the end of my thumb bends back naturally, but you may need to develop the muscle to perfect this position.

Ideally the bridge should be between 9 inches and 12 inches from the white ball. This will, of course, depend on the position of the white ball on the table and where the other balls are in relation to it. Adjustment will have to be

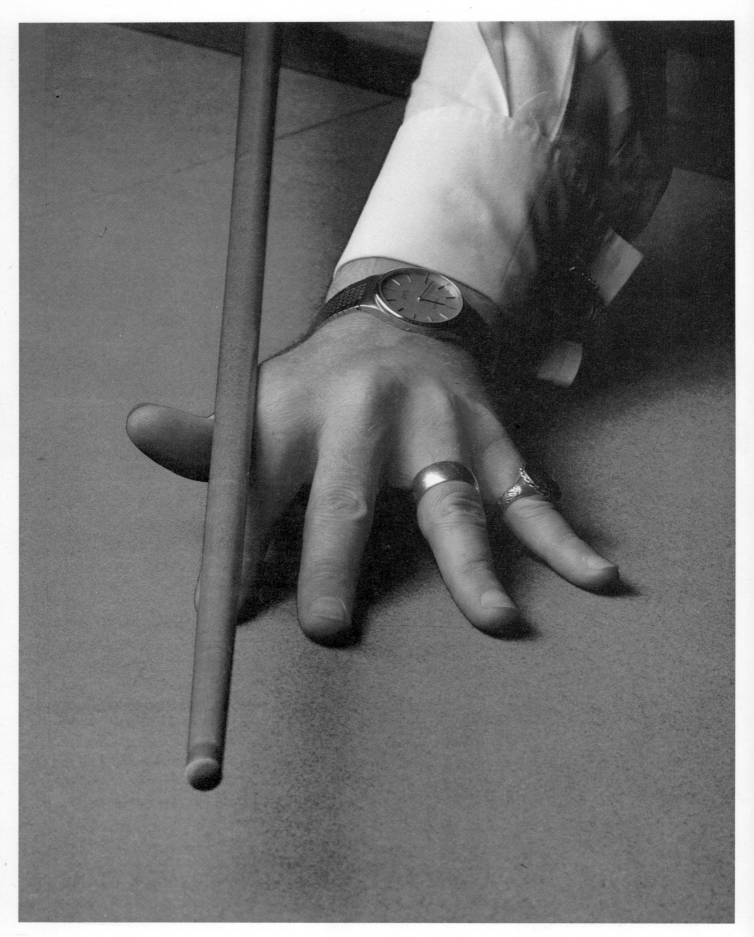

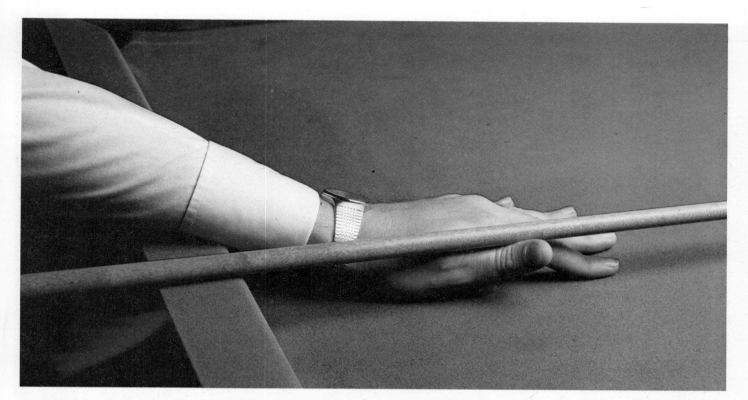

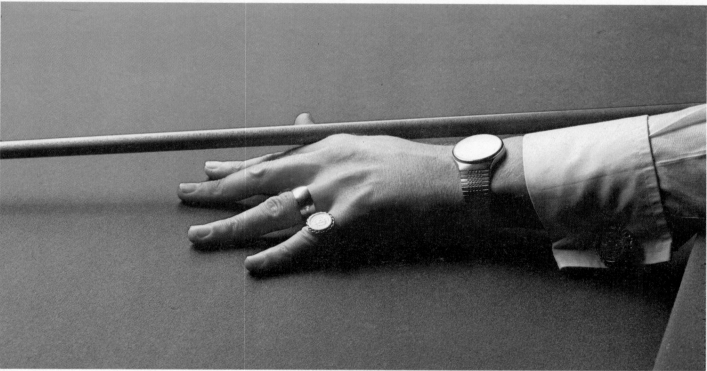

The bridge of course plays a vital part in accurate cueing and, because in virtually all cases it should take a lot of the body weight, it must be firm and solid. This you can achieve by spreading the fingers out over the cloth. Note how the thumb and forefinger create a deep 'V' through which the cue travels, with the forefinger helping to keep it on line. The knuckles raise up automatically as you grip the cloth with the tips of the fingers.

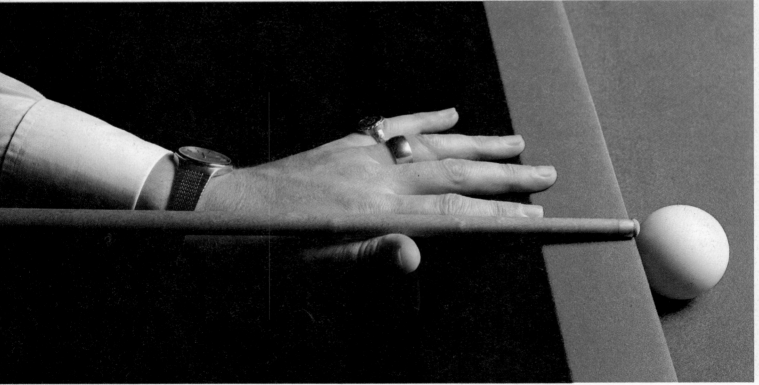

Top: I normally only use the loop bridge when cueing along the cushion. You will see how in this case the forefinger loops over the cue to control it.
Above: Bridging on the edge of the table when the white ball is close to the cushion is never easy, since the fingers provide your only support on the table. You still need, however, to make the bridge as solid as possible.

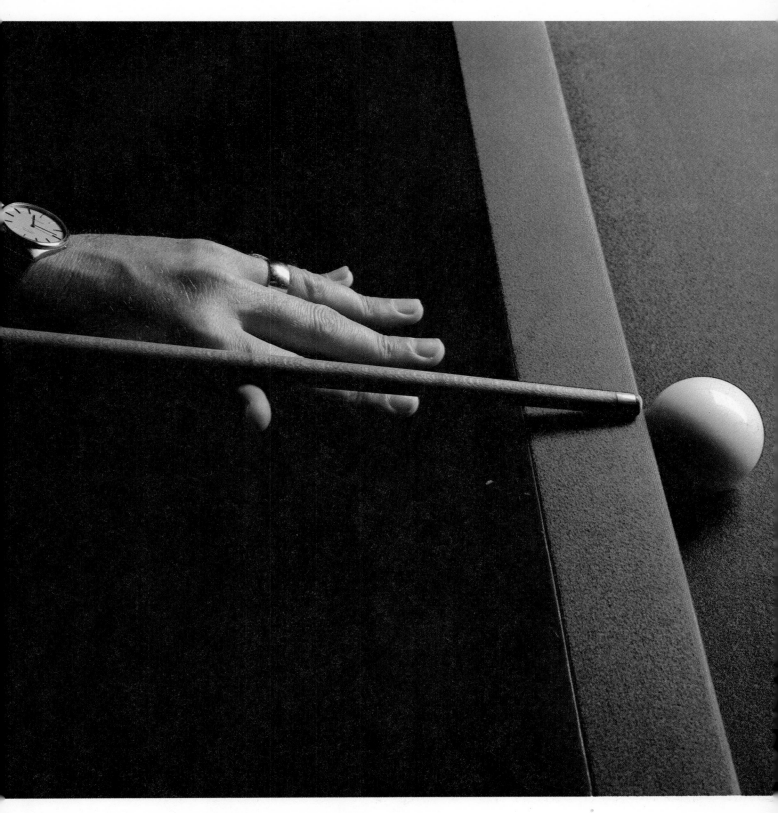

If you need a longer back swing to play a more powerful shot, you will have to bring the fingers back to the edge of the table. Because in this position they provide even less support, there is a great tendency for the bridge hand to move and, as a result, offer even less control over the shot. Experiment to find the most stable bridge, but whenever possible avoid playing power shots from off the cushion since these are particularly difficult and dangerous.

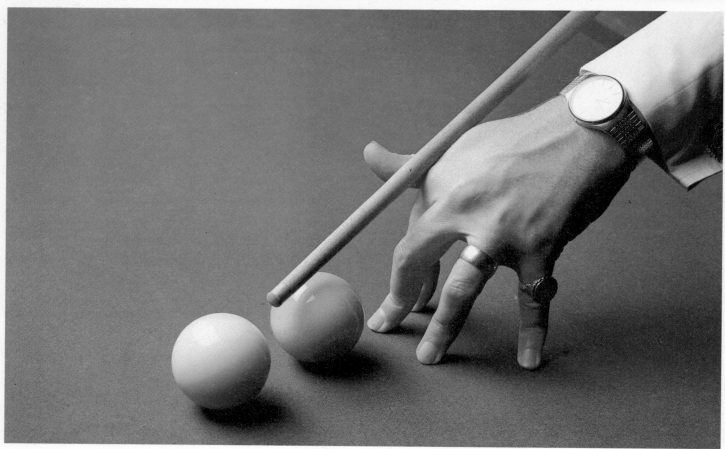

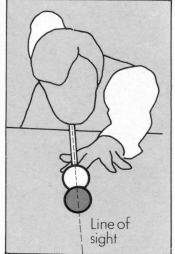

Line of sight

Left: There are occasions when you have to bridge over a ball or group of balls to play the white. In this situation the only contact the bridge has with the table is through the fingertips, and it is therefore far less stable than with normal bridging. For this reason, you should always avoid playing an adventurous shot from this position.

made if it is nearer than this to the cushion, or if there are other balls in the way and you have to bridge over them. This distance does vary from player to player, but you do not want to be much closer than 9 inches or further away than 12 inches.

The height of the bridge can be altered, depending on where on the white ball you want to strike, either by raising the hand slightly or dropping the thumb. In some cases

players actually turn the hand over slightly to lower their bridge. I will come back to this later, when I talk about top and back spin. For the ordinary, plain ball shot the bridge should be at a height where the cue runs through parallel to strike the white ball in the centre.

Since the cue is guided through the bridge, it is vital that there is no movement here – and particularly so if you are playing a power shot. Then you must make sure that your fingers grip the cloth very firmly.

The principle of bridging is to achieve a firm but comfortable position on the table, so that the cue can travel through the bridged hand smoothly and at the correct height. And this is true wherever you have to bridge – whether flat on the table, on the cushion or over another ball.

There are so many variations of bridges, depending on the position of the white ball on the table, that I do not intend to list every one. You will need to experiment yourself, bearing in mind the points I have just made about the bridge. Some people prefer to use the loop bridge, where the cue runs under the forefinger, and in certain situations it is necessary in order to ensure sufficient control of the cue. You must practise the different positions and work out which are the most comfortable – yet firm – ways of bridging to suit the situation.

In talking about the bridge, you must not forget the left arm. Again, the position of this part of the body does vary from player to player. According to many experts the left arm should be thrust out in a straight line over the table – and I think this is probably necessary for those players without an obvious natural ability for the game. I am a compact, but loose, player and prefer to have my left arm slightly bent and resting on the table. One advantage of this position is that it gives more stability to the bridge hand.

Sighting

You should always aim to sight down the cue with both eyes – with your chin over the cue. And this is where the sideways stance comes into effect, so that your right arm,

head and sighting are all in line with the cue and the line of the shot. Having squared up to the shot, the final body movement involves a slight twist of the hips so that the cue just brushes your body. This will help prevent the cue going off line as it moves back and forth.

This is in strict contrast to sighting with a gun, for example, where only one eye is used to line up the target. Having said that, I should point out that some players have sighted with just one eye – Rex Williams and Joe Davis, for example, who both used the left eye.

Using a rest

Although this does take in cue control, the rest acts as an extension to the bridge, when it is impossible to get near enough to the white ball with your bridge hand.

Because of the way in which you have to hold the cue and the altered position of the body, which does not allow you to get your head right over the cue and therefore sight accurately, you have less control over the shot. Do not, therefore, attempt any ambitious shots with the rest. Keep them as simple as possible to avoid making mistakes.

When using the rest, I grip the cue about an inch or so from the end with my thumb underneath and the forefinger and second finger on top. The third finger gives a little

Left: You will need the rest when you cannot comfortably reach the white ball. Note the angled position of the rest. Above: You will have to use the spider to cue over another ball. Compare the upright stance in this situation.

support to the side of the cue. Some players keep the hand behind the butt and use the fingers to support either side of the cue, but this grip does not suit me.

With this grip the elbow points out to the side and the movement of the forearm is therefore a sideways one.

I always place the rest at an angle to the line of the shot so I can distribute the weight of my body more evenly and over a wider area. I feel too cramped when the rest is directly under the cue. The position of my feet changes, too, for shots with the rest. It is virtually the reverse of the normal stance, with the left foot pointing sideways and the right foot virtually in line with the shot. This gives me the front-on position I need so that I can sight over the top of the cue.

The problem with the sideways action of the cue is that there is no longer anything to help keep the cue on line. Normally it would brush gently against the side of the body. This is why it is much harder to bring the cue through on a straight line when using the rest.

Unless I need to hit the white ball well above centre, I always use the rest 'short way up'. If you use it 'tall way up', you may find yourself digging at the white ball and putting

swerve on it by mistake. This is the main problem with the spider, which is designed to bridge over another ball. Effectively, you can only hit the top part of the white ball and so your range of shots here is even more limited.

Your technique

As with any sport, it is far better if you can co-ordinate your movements naturally. However, not everyone will drop into the necessary positions and adopt the various techniques naturally. To start with you will probably find you have to control parts of the body to a degree. But with practice you should eventually be able to achieve a relatively comfortable position.

Basically, as long as you can bring your cue through in a straight line every time, it does not matter how you achieve this. In fact, when I line up for the shot, my right shoulder is not quite in line with the cue. But I still bring the cue through in a straight line. You must experiment with the techniques and see what suits you.

So if you are picking up the cue for the first time – and even if you are not – go up to the table and get down as if to play a shot. Check all the positions of the body against my technique and see how far out yours are from mine. I think this is a better way than trying to imitate all the positions I mentioned in turn, since all will be strange to you. It may be that you adopt some of the right positions naturally and only need to correct a few. At the end of the day, the right stance depends on whether you feel comfortable in a certain position and whether you are hitting the ball correctly – in a straight line.

Since I have taken up playing golf, I have been studying instructional books. And I often think I must be doing it wrong if I am not doing it the way they tell me. But that, as with snooker, is not quite right. If the golf ball goes where you intend it to go, then it is not that important whether you are doing it exactly as the textbook says you should.

A final word on this section of technique – and an important one. I am afraid everyone tries to run before they can walk, and this goes for snooker as much as any other game. I cannot stress enough that you have got to get the stance and body position at the table right before you start thinking about potting a ball. When you stop to think about it, if you do not get these basics right, you will only be hindering possible improvement. That is not to say that within a year or so you may not learn to play reasonably well. But if you concentrate on getting the basics right, it could have been six months.

Cue control

Chapter: 4
Cue control

Having, I hope, mastered the techniques of approaching the table and adopting the correct — or most effective — stance, you are now ready to consider the next control. This is all about bringing the cue through in a straight line to strike the white ball on the spot you have selected for the shot. This may not sound too difficult, but it is vitally important that you master the various stages of the cue action to ensure you strike the white ball accurately and consistently. Most people assume they are striking the white ball where their eyes are telling them to, but very often this is not the case.

At this stage, you must remember that only the right arm, wrist, eyes and cue move. Everything else must stay perfectly still during the cue action. There are six stages that make up the cue action — feathering, back swing, pause, hit, follow-through and stop — and in these lies the secret of timing as you play each shot. When working at the technique involved in these six stages of cue action, you can concentrate on feathering, the back swing and pause individually. But there is no way you can divide up the hit, follow-through and stop. If you try to break these up into separate actions, you will destroy your timing.

Remember that it is easy enough to have everything in line while the whole body is still. The difficulties arise when you start to move the cue and it is vital that you have mastered the basic technique of getting the body in the correct position so that you can trace the faults if you fail to hit the white ball where you want. If you miss a perfectly straight shot and you are in line and have the basics right, then the problem lies in one of the following:
● You have not sighted up correctly.
● Your technique is out and the cue is slightly off line.
● The cue is going off line during the cue action.

The main fault with the more experienced player is normally that the cue travels through off line. With the beginner, the first two faults are likely to have contributed as well.

Feathering
The feathers are the initial movements of the cue up to the white ball — if you like, the build-up to the actual hit. You will find it is the same in golf, where the club is brought up to the ball several times before the back swing and hit, and similarly in tennis where the ball is bounced and then 'shown' to the racquet before the serve.

This build-up, which lasts until you decide it is time to hit the cue ball, is essential to help you get your rhythm and timing right for whichever shot you want to play.

When it comes to feathering, all players differ. Some hardly feather at all, while others — like myself — have very long feathers. Not everyone would agree with long feathers and claim there is more room for the cue to move off the required straight line. But I find it suits my technique. But, however you feather, the point is that you must always do it the same way. This means the length of each feather and the number of feathers before each shot should be the same.

I have been lucky to have had use of video for much of my professional career, so I can watch myself playing and see where I am going wrong — something players in the past could not do. This has helped me a tremendous amount. And the one thing I have noticed particularly is that when I am playing well, my feathers are always the same. And they are never the same when I am playing badly. And this is true of all the players I have watched.

Of course, when you are playing, you probably never think about it or notice it. But if you check — or get somebody else to watch — you will find you can always tell whether you are playing well or badly by the feathers. The number and length will always be the same when you are in top form, but will more often than not vary when you are slightly off your game. By feathering in exactly the same way for each shot, you will find the rhythm comes more easily and you will get the timing right. And this is because, with the same length for each feather, the cue travels the same distance each time. If your rhythm and timing changes, this will affect your cue action — and, in turn, the shot.

You always start feathering from the rest position — that is with the forearm of the right arm in a vertical position and the cue, of course, as near horizontal as possible. When I am feathering, the cue tip almost touches the ball. Some players, like Ray Reardon and Cliff Thorburn, feather short of the white ball. If you practise feathering a lot, you will find you get really close to the white ball when you are playing well — and further away when you are not. I will do four long feathers and then two short ones before I bring the cue back to the pause position. However, as I have said, you do not have to feather in exactly the same way as any other player — as long as you remember the same way each time.

When you do practise feathering, you will find it is very difficult to go right up to the white ball and the tendency is to stop too far back. I do not believe that you can get the rhythm and timing right if you do this. It is far better to hit the white ball a few times by mistake than to shorten your feathers to prevent this happening.

While working at getting your feathers right, do not forget that the body must be perfectly still, except for the right arm. And make sure the cue is going through as horizontally as possible. The longer the swing, the more a 'pumping-type' action will come into effect.

Below: The forward and backward positions of my feathers for a medium pace shot. Note how close I go to the white ball. Right: This shows the difference between the back swing for a normal pace shot and that for a power shot, where because I pull the cue tip back as far as I can into the 'V', it is more difficult to bring the cue through in a straight line.

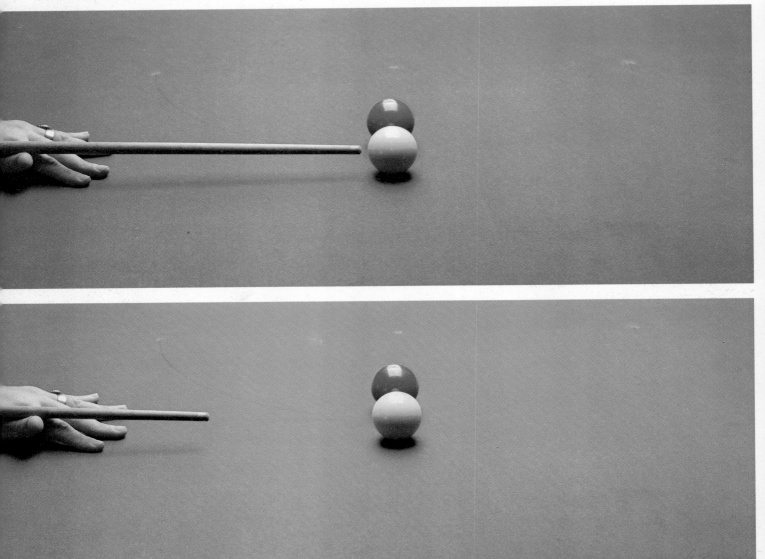

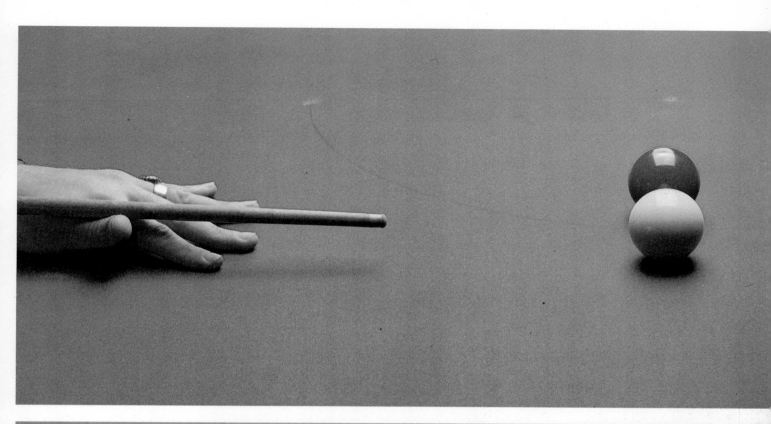

The back swing

The length of the back swing, coupled with the speed of cue delivery, will decide the strength of the stroke. Depending on how far back you bring the cue, certain aspects of technique already mentioned have to change slightly. When you pull the cue back the maximum distance, notice how the wrist bends back slightly and the knuckles are at an angle and no longer parallel. There is no way with maximum back swing that you can keep everything on the horizontal.

One point to remember is that the further back you bring the cue, the greater the chance of error in the cue action. Because the cue has to travel that much further to hit the white ball, there is a lot more room for mistakes.

Many experts will tell you that you should shorten the back swing to cut out the possibility of error. I do not agree

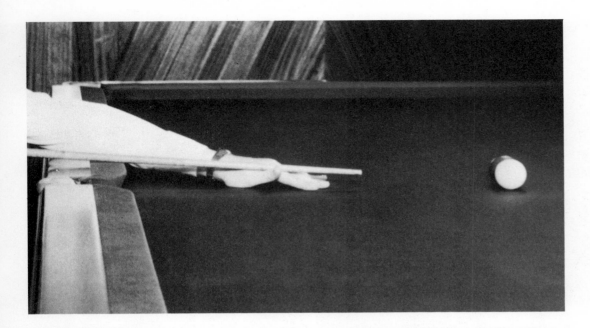

This sequence shows you the position of the cue tip at the pause (end of the back swing), at the hit and after the follow-through, when I am playing a shot at medium pace.

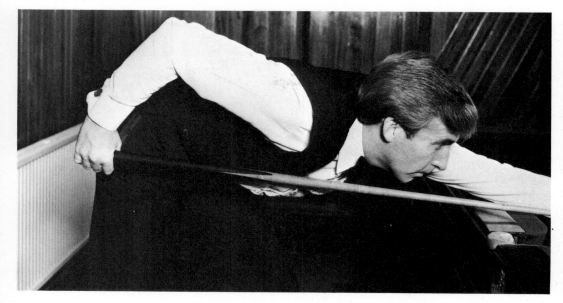

This is the pause, hit and follow-through sequence showing the position of the back arm and wrist at each stage when I am playing a medium pace shot. Note how the line of the knuckles changes at each stage – from being angled down, then straightening up and finally pointing upwards on the follow-through. Throughout this sequence the shoulder must remain steady, although you can see how the elbow drops a little on the follow-through.

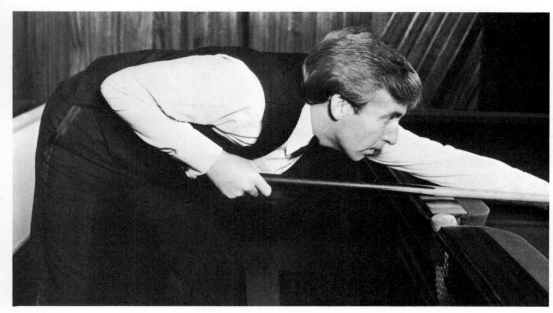

with that. Obviously you must never take the cue back further than you have to for the desired strength of the shot. But the amount of back swing will be dictated by the strength a particular shot needs at the time.

It is all very well to say you should cut down the back swing for all shots, but that would restrict your range of strokes too much. I do not believe you should purposely restrict yourself in this way just to achieve greater accuracy. If the shot requires a great deal of power, then you must go for the maximum back swing.

If you shorten your back swing and try to bring the cue through very fast to achieve maximum speed on the white ball, in my mind that is worse than bringing the cue all the way back and coming through more slowly. I believe in the end you will get more accuracy in the shot by using a longer, slower action than by using a shorter, quicker action. By shortening the back swing and bringing the cue through more quickly, you will lose the rhythm and timing in the shot and you are far more likely to snatch at the white ball.

The problems that arise with having to hit the ball harder are highlighted when you play on a very slow table, since this is the worst thing to knock your cue off line. That is why I think it is rubbish to say that a good player should be able to handle all conditions. You could say that you should be able to play on the carpet. While the hard shot should be part of your repertoire of shots, if you have to play it all the time it will restrict your game – as it does that of the most skilful players.

To play a hard shot does not necessarily mean you should speed up your cue action. In fact it is very important not to bring the cue back too quickly. If you speed up this part of the cue action, you will tend to rush the hit as well. In effect, you lose the pause and speed up the delivery. This is a common fault, just in the same way you will tend to slow down the hit as you shorten the back swing and lengthen the pause. Every movement seems to be exaggerated.

What you must remember is that the way you bring the cue back will dictate what happens to the rest of the cue action. People tend to think that because they are bringing the cue back away from the white ball it does not matter. But the back swing is a very important part of the cue action and affects the final stages, including how you hit the white ball.

The pause
This is an equally crucial part of the cue action and, like feathering, is essential for timing and control of the shot. Drawing an analogy with other sports, again snooker is no different in this respect. There is a certain place where you have got to stop momentarily to come through with the hit. It happens in golf at the top of the back swing – and equally in tennis or cricket – and it happens in football too. There is a pause in dart-throwing, as well, that split second before you release the dart.

The pause comes at the end of the back swing, before you bring the cue forward to strike the white ball. And, as with feathering, it will always be the same when you are playing well. Within reason, the length of the pause does not matter. Steve Davis has one of the longest pauses, whereas Doug Mountjoy claims he does not pause at all; in fact he does, but it is not pronounced.

Of course, at this stage in the cue action, everything must be balanced and perfectly still before you hit. Apart from the eyes, nothing must move until you bring the cue forward to strike the white ball. And remember, once through the pause there is no going back on the shot.

The hit, follow-through and stop
Whatever the type of shot you are playing, you must be positive with the hit. Even if you are playing a gentle shot, you still need a clean, firm contact between the tip of the cue and the white ball. This is where the feathering and pause help, by controlling the rhythm and timing for the shot.

As with the feathering and back swing, the only part of the body that should be moving is the right arm, which should pivot at the elbow as you bring the cue through. The position of the wrist will change as you come through on the shot, straightening out as the forearm reaches the vertical position and then opening slightly as you hit the white ball and follow through.

The important thing to remember with the cue action is that when the tip strikes the white ball, the forearm must be in a vertical position – although this need not be exact. The problem with a lot of players is that they strike the ball either before or after the forearm has reached this position, which almost certainly means they are either standing too close in relation to the white ball or too far away from it. And if the cue does not come through parallel, they will end up hitting the white ball in a slightly downward or upward motion.

The extent of the follow-through depends on the type of shot you are playing and I will discuss this when we get on to control of the cue ball. Equally it varies from player to

52

Here you can see the sequence from the pause through the hit to the follow-through full side-on. Notice that the only part of the body that moves here is the back arm, which comes to the vertical at the hit and drops slightly on the follow-through. Note, too, how close the chin is to the cue when striking the white ball.

The longer the back swing, the more the grip has to open out to enable you to keep the cue as horizontal as possible. You will need to extend the back swing the harder you want to play the shot – and you should do this to gain the desired effect rather than speed up your cue action.

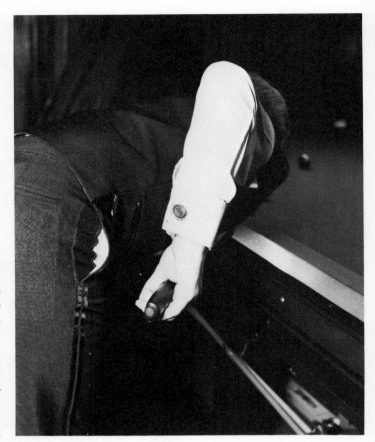

player. I have a particularly long follow-through, which is necessary with my timing. So do many of the top professionals – for example, Ray Reardon, Alex Higgins, Tony Knowles and Doug Mountjoy. Steve Davis, on the other hand, has a much shorter follow-through while Tony Meo has a very short cue action with virtually no follow-through at all.

Again, you can check your action against that of the top players and practise shortening or lengthening your follow-through. But their way is not necessarily the right way for you. You must try it out and see what suits your cue action.

But the follow-through is still part of the cue action – and a necessary one – which is linked with the other techniques to the control and timing of the shot. So the same principle of keeping the cue horizontal applies here, although with extreme power shots the cue is bound to lift slightly at the end of the follow-through.

Obviously you have to stop the cue on the follow-through somewhere. Because this last stage in the cue action is something that a natural player would never think about but just does, it is often neglected. For the top players it is something they do automatically – stopping the cue at the right time for the right stroke.

Where and when you stop the cue will depend on the speed at which you deliver the cue, coupled with the type of spin – if any – you want to put on the white ball.

The stop becomes more important when you want to screw back the white ball than with any other type of shot, since it will determine the amount of 'bite' you get on the white. The screw back, which I will talk about later, is still a full stroke. But by stopping the cue at the right time, the tip will hold on to the white for a while to enable you to achieve maximum spin on the white with the minimum of effort.

With this type of shot, timing is all important. When people attempting this shot make the white jump, it means they have stopped the cue too early, before it has gone through with the stroke. Equally, if they do not stop the cue in time, they will not get the required amount of back spin – if any at all – on the white.

When and where to stop the cue is something you will only learn with practice and experience, by varying the power of the shot and judging the different effects on the white ball.

But you must always remember that the stop cannot be separated from the other final stages of cue action – the hit and the follow-through. The three must be practised together as part of one complete action. And the stop

should become a natural part of this action. Once you start thinking about where you should stop the cue, it becomes very difficult indeed to get the desired effect on the white ball.

Hitting the cue ball
Once you have got the cue moving back and forth in a straight line – and remember this part of the technique can take up to six months to master, even if you play every day – you can then think about hitting the white ball in a straight line.

There is a story I was once told by a very close friend Mario Berni, a highly respected student of snooker, about Horace Lindrum, which illustrates perfectly the point I want to make here. When he was learning to play, his uncle gave him a white ball and said: 'When you've learned to hit that properly, I'll give you another ball to hit.' Lindrum practised with that one ball all day, every day, for two weeks before his uncle gave him a second ball.

It is hard enough learning to bring the cue through in a straight line. When you put a ball there, it gets more difficult. Introduce a second ball and aim to hit that into a pocket and it gets as difficult as it can be. Unfortunately beginners tend to think it is very easy, but it is not.

My whole philosophy on coaching is learning to hit the white ball in a straight line, since whatever the potting angle the white must always travel in a straight line to the object ball. This is why you must master this first if you eventually want to pot balls consistently.

The following set of exercises will help you develop this technique of hitting the white ball in a straight line. Put the white ball on the brown spot, which is the centre spot on the baulk line. What you are aiming to do here is to hit the white up and down the spots in the centre of the table — that is the blue, pink and black spots.

The point here is that if you have adopted the correct position at the table and you have everything right with your cue action, you do not even have to look at the white ball. If your cue comes through in a straight line and hits the white ball in the centre, it should travel up the table over the spots, strike the top cushion and come back over the spots.

You should not regard the actual striking of the white ball as a separate stage of the shot. In effect the white ball will travel up the table because it is in the way of the cue coming through in a straight line. Once you start to think of the hit, your mind is diverted from the things it should be concentrating on — the stages of the cue action we have already discussed.

Correct sighting for this shot will depend on whether you are standing in the right position or not. If you are not dead in line, the white ball will not travel in a straight line over the spots. Check too that the cue is moving along this line of sight.

Having positioned yourself correctly, sighted accurately and brought the cue through in a straight line to hit the white ball in the centre, the white has got to run in a straight line over the blue, pink and black spots, hit the top cushion and come back down in the same line. Hitting straight is a very difficult exercise to master and will take a long time, so do not be disheartened when you do not get it right first time.

If the white does not travel in a straight line over the spots, where have you gone wrong? Of course, it could be that your position and sighting were out in the first place. If the cue ball runs over the spots on the way up the table, but travels off line after hitting the top cushion, this means you have not hit the ball in the centre. In fact, what you have inadvertently done is to put side spin on the white. I will be looking at this later. If the white ball fails to run over the spots on its way up the table, it is probably because your cue did not come through in a perfect straight line.

The secret here is to keep your eye on the tip of the cue and never on the white ball. If you concentrate on the ball and then look at the cue, you may think it has come through straight when in fact it may have straightened up with the follow-through. By watching just the tip of the cue you should be able to tell whether it has come through off line or, as sometimes happens, it has gone off line and then straightened up towards the end of the cue action.

So, for these exercises, ignore the white ball and concentrate on the tip of the cue. When everything has gone right, the cue will go through in a dead straight line and is bound to hit the white in the centre and send it up over the spots.

What about the pace of the shot? Well, the harder you try to strike the white ball in this exercise, the more difficult it is to hit the centre spot on the ball. This is perfectly illustrated by the fact that after the white hits the top cushion it will probably come back way off the brown spot. This exercise will exaggerate any error in the cue action.

So the lesson to be learned here is never put more effort into the stroke than is needed. Pace is a combination of the speed with which the cue comes through to the hit and the length of the back swing — and it takes a long time to get the feel of this, to understand pace and to be able to measure it accurately.

It is a common fault of the beginner to use more pace than length when trying to hit hard. By playing the shot more quickly, the tendency is to jerk at it — rather than lengthen the back swing and keep the action smooth. I will be looking more at power shots when we come to cue ball control.

The aim for beginners with these exercises is to hit the white ball with enough pace for it to strike the top cushion and come back over the brown spot. That will be enough to start with. Once you become efficient at that and can do it three times on the trot, then you can try hitting the white ball a bit harder and work up to maximum pace, but still getting the white to come back within two inches either side of the brown spot. You will never get any better than that. It is as good as I can get it. With maximum pace, there is no way the white will come back over the brown spot every time.

So, to recap, the object of this exercise is to learn to stand in the right place, sight correctly, deliver the cue in a straight line and make the white ball travel in a straight line. Once you have mastered this at varying speeds you can move on to the next exercise — putting a ball (the object ball) in the way of the white.

For this exercise, put the white ball on the brown spot again and place the blue ball in line with the spots about a foot up the table from the white. You now have an object ball in the way. The tip of the cue should still strike the white ball in the centre and this should then hit the blue ball and send it in a straight line to the top cushion and back down the table to kiss the white ball in the same line.

This is a much harder exercise to perform, but if — as a beginner — you can master it within three months you are

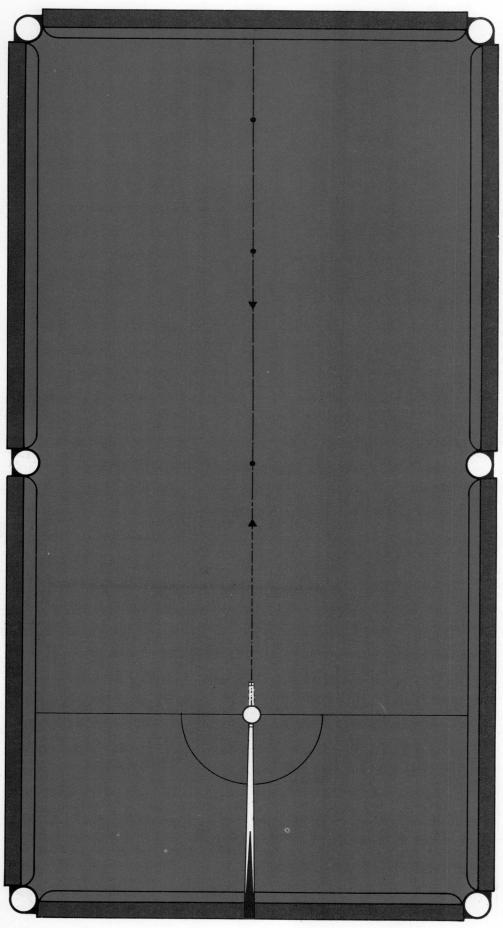

This is the most basic and important exercise in snooker – practising to hit the white ball in a straight line. Place the white on the brown spot and, with a medium pace stroke, try getting the white to travel up the table over the blue, pink and black spots to the top cushion and back over the same spots. When you practise this, remember you should not watch the white ball. Provided that you have sighted up correctly, are cueing in a straight line and hit the white in the centre, the ball should travel over the spots. What you should be watching is the cue tip, since only by doing this will you see whether the cue is coming through on line or not.

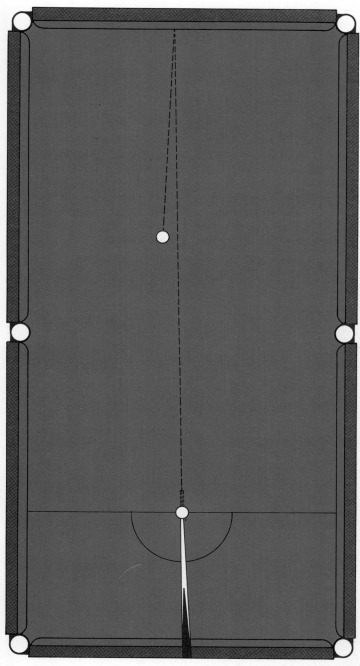

When playing up and down the spots, one of the common faults is not maintaining a straight cue delivery throughout the shot. You have sighted correctly and got the stance and basic techniques right, but the cue deviates off line during the cue action. The effect of this is to put some side spin on the ball, which you have hit off-centre. What happens here is that the white travels up the table over the spots, but comes off the top cushion at a slight angle and obviously does not travel back over the spots.

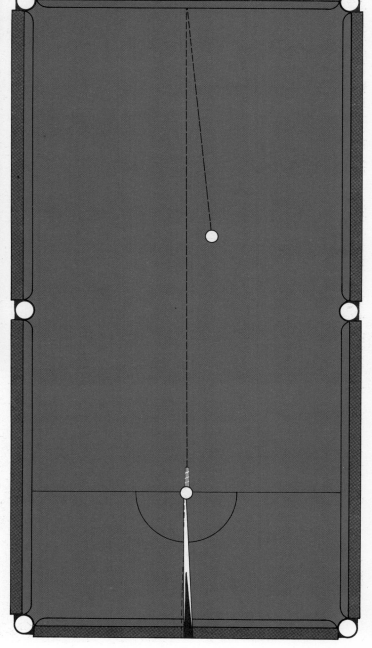

Another common fault with this exercise is incorrect sighting. Although you think you are aiming the cue in a straight line over the spots, the slightest deviation off this line is enough to make the white miss the brown spot by several inches on its way back down the table. Although the basic techniques and cue delivery are correct, you have been let down by inaccurate sighting.

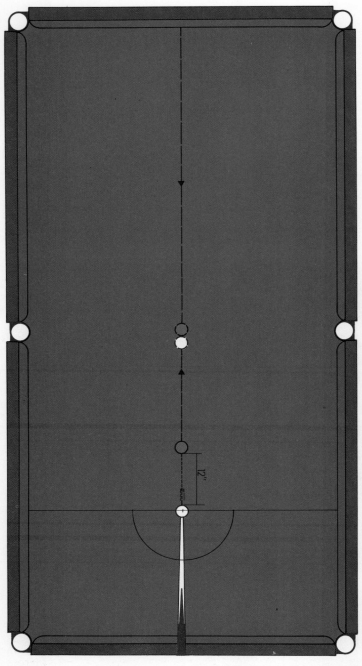

Although working on the same principle as the first exercise, you are now attempting a more advanced exercise by putting a ball in the way. Place the blue about a foot up the table from the white, in line with the spots, and play the white with medium pace again. What you are aiming to do is to send the blue ball up the table and back over the spots to kiss the white ball around the blue spot.

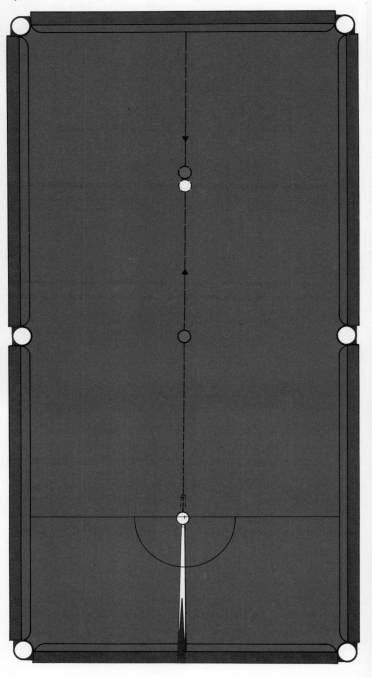

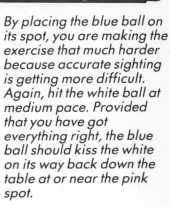

By placing the blue ball on its spot, you are making the exercise that much harder because accurate sighting is getting more difficult. Again, hit the white ball at medium pace. Provided that you have got everything right, the blue ball should kiss the white on its way back down the table at or near the pink spot.

making great progress.

As with the previous exercises, it is no good doing this successfully once. You must be able to do it three times on the trot before you go on to the next exercise.

Now put the blue ball on its spot, with the white on the brown spot. The object again is to take the blue up to the top cushion and back down to kiss the white. This may not appear to be any different from the previous exercise, but the greater the distance between the white and the object ball, the harder the sighting becomes. Of course, the action is just the same. The easiest way to illustrate this is to try potting the white ball into a pocket. You will find you can do this virtually every time. Put another ball in the way and somehow it is totally different.

In a way, it is similar to aiming at a target with a gun. You will find it easy to hit from a short distance. But increase the range and it becomes that much harder. Obviously we are not talking about the same kind of distances on a snooker table, but it is a fact of life that long range shots are missed far more regularly than closer shots. They demand much more accuracy in the striking of the white ball because it has to travel that much further before it hits the object ball — and so the margin for error is increased.

Pace is again important in these exercises. Think when you do them whether you are hitting the white ball as soft as you could but still getting the balls to kiss. There should be just enough pace in the shot to bring the blue back to the white.

And throughout these exercises, concentrate on the tip of the cue. Did it come through in a straight line or did it go off line at any stage? This will help tell you where you are going wrong. If you hit the white off line, there is no way the blue will kiss it on the way back.

It is most important that you use these exercises and those covered later in the book, to experiment with your technique. Never try experimenting during a game or in competition play. Working on your technique must be kept to solo practice.

Having mastered these exercises, it is now time to look at potting the ball.

Potting in a straight line

Whether you are playing a straight pot or trying to pot at an angle, the key point to remember is that you will always be hitting the white ball in a straight line. This is why the straight line exercises are so vital — and basic to the whole game of snooker.

The first hurdle to overcome when trying to pot a ball is to be able to question what your eyes tell you. What I mean is that when you go to pot a ball, your eyes will tell you the ball must go in the pocket. When it misses the pocket by several inches, the tendency is to go on trying the pot in the hope that the ball will somehow eventually go in the right direction. You must stop and think to yourself: 'Why did it miss the pocket and what must I do to get the ball to go the same distance in the other direction — into the pocket?'

Always start off in a straight line, with the white and object ball in a direct line with the pocket. This way you can forget about potting the object ball and concentrate on your technique, which is the reason why you missed the pot in the first place.

The trouble is that everybody likes to see a ball moving. Take pinball machines or roulette, for example. But to achieve really accurate movement of the ball in snooker, you must spend a lot of time thinking about all the techniques involved right up to the actual striking of the white ball.

The exercise to practise for potting in a straight line is as follows: Taking the diagonal line between opposite corner pockets on the table, place the white ball on the baulk line and the blue ball on the same diagonal about a foot up the table from the white. To pot the blue into the top corner pocket you must hit the white ball in the centre. Because the blue is in the same straight line to the pocket it should go in — if all the basic techniques are correct.

What happens, then, if you fail to pot the blue? You must revert to the basic things that could have gone wrong. Were you sighting correctly? Were you lined up correctly for the shot, through the centre of the white ball? And did the cue come through straight along the line of sight? Watching the tip is still all important and you should tell by this whether you came through in a straight line or not. If you have difficulty judging this, then get a friend to stand at the other end of the table over the pocket to see whether your line and action are straight or not. And do not forget to check the basics, such as the position of the feet and whether the head is still and directly over the cue.

Potting at an angle

Having spent time practising hitting the white ball in a straight line — and potting in a straight line — you are now looking at the situation where to pot the object ball you have to deflect it at an angle in order to get it into the pocket.

This exercise is to practise potting a ball in a straight line. Put the white on the baulk line and the blue about a foot away both on the diagonal line between opposite corner pockets. The principle is the same as before – hitting the centre of the white, with both balls travelling in a straight line. Remember you must not keep your eyes on the white.

Always watch the tip of the cue during the hit and follow-through so you can see where you went wrong if you fail to pot the brown.

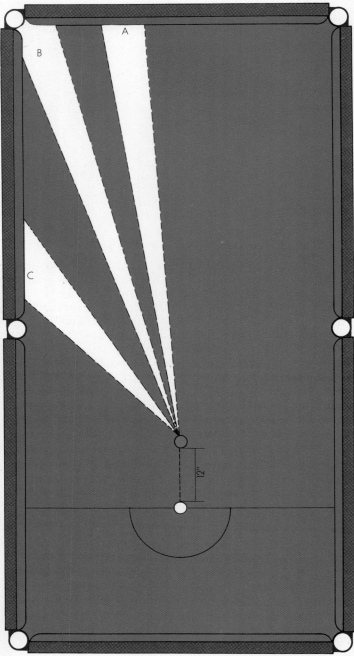

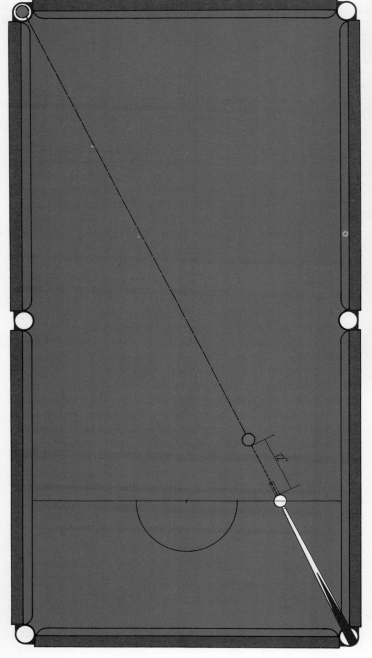

This is a useful exercise to practise potting angles and to see where the white will travel after contact with the blue when you play a plain shot – that is, without putting any spin on the white ball. With a threequarter-ball angle the white will travel within white area A, with a half-ball angle white area B and with a quarter-ball angle white area C. Where exactly it goes within these areas will depend on the pace of the shot.

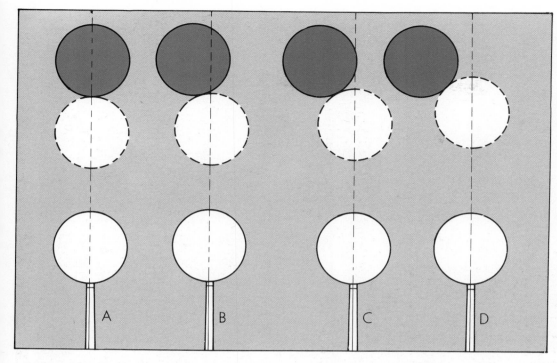

A   B   C   D

It is never easy, when you start playing, to work out exactly where on the object ball the white ball must hit to send it off at a specific angle. It should, however, help you if you can imagine a line through the cue tip and the centre of the white ball onto the object ball. In this case, for a threequarter-ball angle this line would go through a point halfway between the centre and the outside edge of the object ball. For a half-ball angle, the line would go through the outside edge of the object ball. For a quarter-ball angle, the line would go through a point one quarter of a ball's width away from the outside edge.

What you must keep at the back of your mind is that the straight line is still there. Regardless of what angle is needed on the object ball, the contact of the white ball still involves hitting it in a straight line.

It is a natural reaction, when you are faced with an angled pot, to think that suddenly everything has changed. But you must remember that the principle of hitting the white ball onto the object ball is still the same. You must strike the white ball in a straight line.

The main problem now is working out the correct angles for the pot and, therefore, where contact has to be made on the object ball for it to go into the pocket.

You may find it hard to believe, but when I am coaching I am constantly asked: 'How do you make the ball go that way?' So it is imperative that you think about the angle and where you have to hit the object ball before you start.

The easiest way to understand what happens to the object ball when the white ball hits it off centre is to line the two balls up in a straight line and think about what would happen if you hit the white on to a certain side of the object ball. Then try it out and see what happens. Does it go in the direction you expected?

This is far more profitable than trying to pot a ball at an angle first time — and carrying on with the same shot a number of times and still missing the pocket.

When you get down, think about the shot. If you hit the object ball in a certain place, where will it go? Then try out the shot and see where it goes. Bring the balls back and try again at a different angle and see what happens this time. It is only by doing this that you can get a mental picture of how the object ball reacts when hit in a certain place.

Then, when you approach the table to pot the object ball at an angle, having got in your mind a mental picture of the angle, you should be able to work out the correct position before you get down to hit the white ball. After all, by the time you have hit the white ball it will be too late.

The principle behind the technique of potting is to work it all out before you get down to the shot, since the position you eventually adopt will dictate where the white ball will hit

the object ball — and therefore whether or not it ends up in the pocket.

You must remember that there is always a reason why the object ball does not end up in the pocket — and it is not because the pocket has moved or that the ball has suddenly turned square! If you fail to pot a ball, there is something wrong with your technique or you have selected the wrong angle — or possibly both are to blame.

Potting the object ball at an angle depends on the player's eyesight and memory — judging the angle correctly. And one thing that beginners constantly get wrong when they go down to take the pot, is to adjust their stance after deciding that the ball will not go in from the original position.

This does not mean that you have to get up from the table and start again — although you should if any major adjustment has to be made. But you should move as a unit to retain the overall balance required to hit the white ball accurately. The danger of adjusting your position is that you may move the feet slightly, or the head, or alter the bridge in such a way as to affect the cue action.

When you approach the table, first think about where you would stand for a straight pot, since this is always the easiest position to assess. Then think about where you should stand in order to hit the object ball off line — at the required angle — to effect the pot and get down in this position. Once you get down, your potting angle should be determined.

The best way to get used to judging angles is to go back to the straight line exercise mentioned earlier. Put the white ball on the brown spot and the blue ball about a foot up the table in a straight line. Then experiment by hitting the blue ball on either side and watch where it hits the top cushion, making a mental note of the angle each time.

You can follow up this exercise by trying, with the white and blue balls in the same positions, to pot the blue into the bottom pockets. To start with, you will doubtless miss the pot. But see each time how far out you are and make the necessary adjustments to pot the blue. As a beginner you

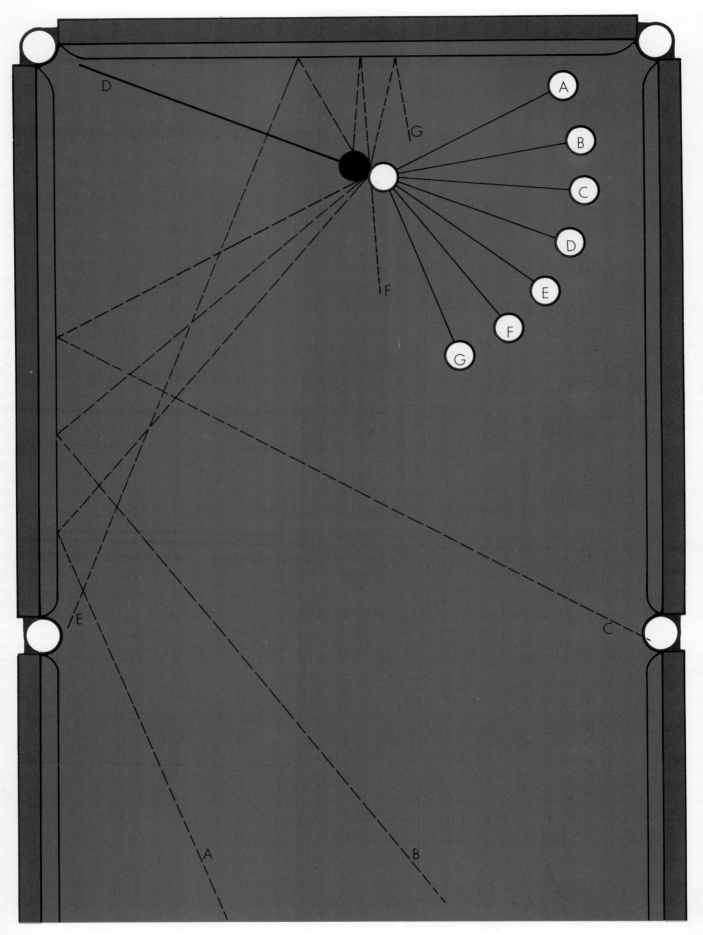

This is another useful exercise to practise potting angles, particularly since potting the black off its spot is one of the most common shots when trying to build up a break. The range of angles is indicated as quarter-ball (A), half-ball (B), threequarter-ball (C), full-ball (D), threequarter-ball (E), half-ball (F) and quarter-ball (G). The diagram shows in which direction the white will travel after a plain-ball shot at each angle. Remember that in each case the white makes contact at exactly the same point on the black and this is the furthest point on the black in a straight line from the centre of the pocket.

will find that the adjustment needed is a lot less than you think it will be. So keep trying until you get it right.

Potting angles

To the beginner it probably seems that the number of different angles for potting are incalculable. In fact there are four basic angles, which crop up all over the table. Obviously slight adjustments will be needed to each of these angles, depending on the exact position of the balls, but wherever you are playing on the table you will be faced with basically one of the four.

The basic potting angles are full ball, three-quarter ball, half ball and quarter ball. All the other angles you may need will be slight adjustments — that is, a bit thinner or a bit thicker. Of course, once you can recognise these you will find potting becomes a very much easier task. But recognition will only come with practice and experience. You must not expect to work out the angles overnight.

And even when you can recognise and sight up correctly for different angle shots, do not assume you will be successful with the shot if you have still not mastered hitting and potting in a straight line. I am afraid it all goes back to basics and it is important to remember this when you miss an angled pot. You tend immediately to assume that because you missed the pot, you must have judged the angle incorrectly. It may well be, however, that your basic technique was at fault and not your judgement.

Having mentioned the four basic angles, how do you line up the white ball with the object ball to ensure you hit the object ball in the correct place?

At this stage, you should always be thinking in terms of centre-ball striking, that is without spin. So what you have to imagine is a line through the cue and the centre of the white ball to the relevant part of the object ball.

Let me explain. For the full ball, the imaginary line would be to the centre of the object ball — that is a straight pot. For a three-quarter-ball pot, the imaginary line would be from the tip of the cue, through the centre of the white ball to a spot a quarter width from the outside edge of the object ball. For a half-ball pot, you should be lining up on a spot just missing the outside edge of the object ball. For a quarter-ball pot you should be aiming at an imaginary spot one quarter of a ball's width away from the outside edge of

the object ball, admittedly not that easy to estimate.

Of course, not all pots will fit neatly into these four categories. Because there will always be variations, however slight, this is not a guaranteed way of potting the ball. And, unfortunately, the eye will barely distinguish between, say, a half-ball and fractionally thicker than a half-ball. At the end of the day, this is down to memory, experience and ability — and, of course, how well you are playing at the time.

Even though I have had years of experience in working out and memorising the angles, I still miss pots sometimes — as do all the top players. Then you have to go back to the techniques and work out where you have gone wrong. It does not matter how many years you have been playing the game. There are always times when your technique is slightly out and lets you down. The important thing is to be able to recognise that this has happened and to go back and adjust it.

One final word on potting angles — and an important reminder. Just because the balls are in different positions in different parts of the table does not mean that the angles are any different. Those quarter-, half- and three-quarter balls are cropping up everywhere, so do not be misled — or put off — by thinking that you have got to learn millions of different shots. You will find that the same shots will recur in varying parts of the table and the main difference will be in the distance between the white ball and the object ball. And remember that whatever the angle needed on the object ball, you will still be hitting the white ball in a straight line.

Potting is all about memorising angles and this only comes with constant practice. You must bear this in mind and not get disheartened because you cannot pot the ball regularly overnight. It is worth considering that it took me 21 years to reach the standard I have now achieved — and I still do not get everything right all the time. And this is why I must stress the need to check your technique all the time.

Never be afraid to question and go back to the basic cue action when things go wrong, since a fault here will affect every shot you play. And unless you can truthfully say that you have mastered the techniques so far, do not expect results from the most advanced aspects of the game I am about to discuss.

Cue ball control

Chapter: 5

Cue ball control

Having looked at the control of the body and the control of the cue, it is now time to go on to control of the cue ball, which is essential if you want to achieve any reasonable standard in snooker. With this control, you will be able to get the white ball into a good position for the next shot — and from there to go on to a sequence of shots and build up a decent break.

To achieve a good position with the white ball, two aspects of the shot are of ultra-importance. The tip of the cue must strike the white ball in the correct spot and you must play the shot with the right amount of pace. Here, of course, I am assuming that all the previous techniques are correct as well.

Spin

The key to controlling the cue ball is spin. I will be concentrating here on two types — the back spin and the top spin. There is, of course, side spin and I will go on to this later. But personally, except in one or two specific cases, I avoid playing this type of spin whenever possible.

The important point to remember about top spin and

This diagram shows the different effects top and back spin have on the white ball. Comparing these with a plain-ball shot (A), when you put top spin on the white (B), which means hitting the top of the white with the cue tip, although the white will travel forward in the usual way, on impact with the object ball the white will pick up momentum from the top spin you put on it. When you put back spin on the white (C), the effect after contact with the object ball is reversed and the white will travel back towards you as the back spin takes effect.

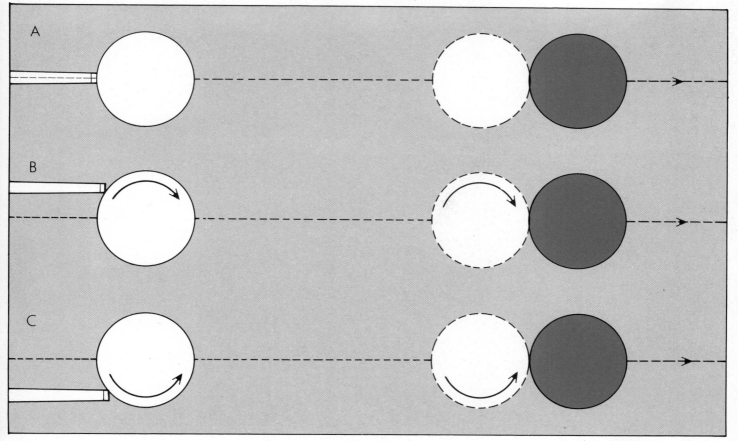

Here you get a player's view of the point of contact on the white when playing a plain-ball (left), top spin (below) and back spin (bottom). Notice that in each case the cue tip is striking on a line down the centre of the white ball.

back spin is that you are still aiming to hit on the imaginary centre line through the white ball. And do not be misled into thinking that because of the different effects you can get from spin there are many different kinds. Most of the effects can be gained by slight variations of the two basic types.

To effect these spins you need, as I have said, to hit the white ball along the centre line. With top spin, this means aiming the cue tip to hit the extreme top centre of the white; with back spin, you must aim to hit the extreme bottom centre of the white.

The best way to understand how to make the white ball spin and what effect this will have is to work at the following exercise: Put the pink ball on its spot and place the white ball on a line from one of the centre pockets to the opposite top corner pocket. This will be a straight line through the pink. The white should be about a foot away from the pink between that and the middle pocket.

It is far better to start practising spins and experimenting with the effects in a straight line. It gets a lot more complicated when the balls are at an angle to the pocket.

If you play a plain ball shot on the white – that is hitting it in the centre with no spin – at medium pace with maximum follow-through, you should pot the pink into the corner pocket and the white should carry on through and run into the same pocket. The best way to judge the pace for this shot is to go back to the straight line exercise with the white on the brown spot.

Medium pace would be when the white travels up the table, back down over the brown spot to the bottom cushion, returns over the brown spot and ends up on the top cushion again.

With the pink and white balls in the same position, play the shot again but this time with extreme top spin. This means hitting the white at the extreme top centre, at medium pace with maximum follow-through again. If you play the shot correctly, the pink will go into the corner pocket and the white should follow it in, this time at a much faster speed.

Now try playing the same pot, but with extreme back spin. Keep to the same pace of shot, but restrict the follow-through to half the maximum. When you strike the bottom of the white ball, people think you cannot follow through; but you can. With this shot the stop comes into effect a lot sooner than with other shots and the actual pace of the cue when you stop the follow-through is all important in how quickly or slowly the white ball will spin back into the centre pocket.

From this you will see that the effect of spin relies heavily on all the other things that come into timing – the feathers, the pause, the hit and the follow-through – and particularly where the stop takes effect. Crisp, accurate striking is equally important. You must hit the white ball along the centre line and the tip must make contact in exactly the right spot to get the desired effect.

The most popular shot for beginners is the screw-back. If the white ball spins back, it does not seem to matter to them what else happens. But when they try the shot, there seems to be a built-in mental fear that the white ball will jump and so the tip comes up before the hit. The white, of course, does not spin back and they wonder why. The fact is that they have not hit the bottom of the ball. You must always remember that balls do not play tricks. If you hit the bottom of the white correctly, it will come back.

There is no secret about playing with back spin. It is simply a question of getting the timing right, hitting the white at the extreme bottom centre and stopping the follow-through at the correct time. This enables the tip to stay on the white for as long as possible so that you get the necessary 'bite' to effect the back spin required. Depending on how you play these, the white ball may stop dead after striking the pink, come back some of the way or, with the right amount of screw back, come back quickly into the centre pocket.

There are a number of things that can go wrong when you attempt the back spin. You may not have hit the white ball low enough. You may not have had enough pace in the shot. You may have followed through too far with the shot and, instead of putting spin on the white, you have in effect just pushed it along the table; in fact, the white ball skids along the bed of the table. The hit must be more like a bite.

Compare the application of spin in table tennis. To get the ball to spin, you have to skim the edge of the ball with the bat. In a way, what you are doing in snooker is skimming the bottom of the white; really, it is just a touch.

It is probably one of the most difficult of all the controls on the cue ball and one that some people never master. In fact it is more accurate to say that nobody masters it – some never play it at all. You have got to get out of your mind the fear that you might jump the white ball, which rarely happens anyway.

The speed at which the cue is delivered and where you stop the follow-through are the key indicators of where most people go wrong on the shot. Provided that the rest of

This side-on view of plain-ball striking (right) and playing with top spin (below) and back spin (bottom) illustrates one very important point about using these types of spin. You must still keep the cue as horizontal as possible. One of the common faults with players attempting the back spin is to dig into the bottom of the ball with an angled cue. Not only can it cause the white to jump, but it will not impart the required back spin on the ball.

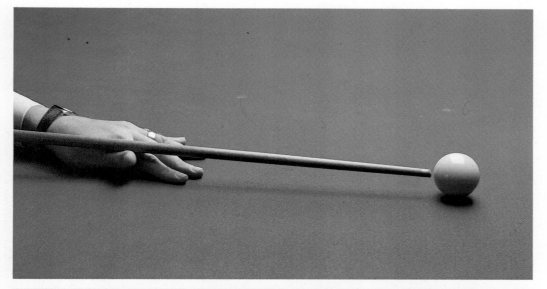

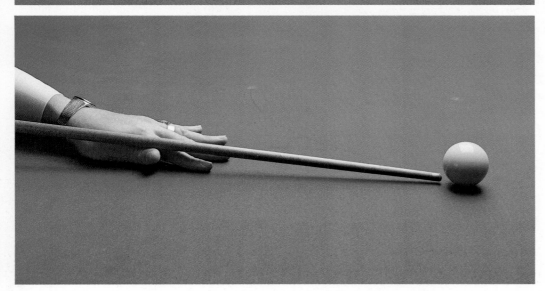

When using top or back spin you will have to alter the height of your bridge to ensure the cue is kept horizontal. Here you can see the position of the bridge for a plain-ball shot (left), the raised bridge when playing with top spin (centre) and the lowered bridge when using back spin (bottom). This is the only correct way of ensuring that you achieve the right point of contact on the white for these types of spin. You must make the necessary adjustments to the level of the cue at both ends to keep it roughly horizontal. The common fault here is to keep the same bridge but either raise or lower the butt of the cue in order to strike the white ball at the top or the bottom. If you do this, you will not be bringing the cue through in a line parallel to the table. At best, you will not get the effect from the spin you wanted; at worst you will either miscue or make the white ball jump off the cloth.

the cue action is correct and the aim is good, you will find you have either brought the cue through too quickly or too slowly – or you have stopped the cue too early or too late.

There is another common fault with the back spin that I am about to come on to, but will mention briefly here. Next time you go into a club, have a look round to see how other players cope with the back spin. You will find that many of them raise the butt of the cue to hit the bottom of the white, rather than lowering their bridge.

Bearing in mind that you should always strive to keep the cue as horizontal as possible, it stands to reason that in order to hit higher up or lower down on the white ball you must alter the height of the bridge. But it is surprising how many people will simply alter the angle of the cue by lifting or lowering the butt.

Basically the bridge is the only part of the body that alters when you play spin. With top spin, the bridge hand must be raised. To achieve this, pull the fingers of your bridge hand towards you slightly to create an arch. This will lift the tip end of the cue and obviously you must raise the butt end as well to keep the cue horizontal.

When playing top spin, the bridge will not be as firm and rigid as with the plain ball (centre striking) shot and you must bear this in mind, since it will to a degree restrict the type of shot you play since you are likely to get a little movement in the hand.

With the back spin, it is just the opposite. You must lower the bridge hand as much as possible and drop the cocked thumb. In order to get the V-shaped groove as low as possible, some players turn the hand slightly. Having lost the use of the thumb as a guide for the cue, your forefinger is now more important than ever and you must use it to help control the cue coming through.

To learn the different effects of top and back spin, you will have to experiment and study what happens each time. Are you hitting the cue ball too high or too low? Are you hitting too hard or too soft? Are you following through too far or not far enough? You have to understand and think about what is happening to the white ball to recognise what is going wrong when you do not get the effect you wanted. If the white ball goes through too far, you have hit it too high or played the shot too slowly. If with top spin the white does not run through far enough, you have hit it too low or too softly – or both. Of course, if it runs off line, then you have not hit it straight to begin with.

Bearing in mind that you have hit the ball in a straight line, or so we must assume, how can you check you are hitting the white ball at the right height? Of course you must check that your bridge hand is high enough or low enough – and you must check whether the cue is coming through horizontally. To do this, look back and watch the gap between the cue and the cushion – or the table. If this remains constant, then the cue must be coming through horizontally. The tendency is to bring the cue up too high, for example, on the back spin shot.

One way of controlling the line of the cue is by bringing your chin down as near as possible to the cue and keeping it there during the cue action. If you lift the cue at all it will touch the chin. And, depending on how low you drop the cue, your knuckles will graze the cushion or the table.

Stun

This is basically a variation of the back spin and, when played accurately, will enable the white ball to stop dead on impact with the object ball. This is a very useful shot to be able to play, since you can guarantee where the white ball will finish up after the shot.

But it is a very difficult shot and is therefore not used a great deal in the modern game. It is the only shot on the snooker table where absolutely no follow-through is used. To play it, you need to hit the white slightly below centre at medium pace and stop the cue on impact with the white.

It will need a lot of practice to get any kind of consistency into this shot. If the white runs on after impact with the object ball, you have hit it too high. If the white screws back after impact you have hit it too low. And remember, there is no follow-through with this shot.

Stun run-through

To give you an idea of how valuable this shot is, in the professional game up to 75 per cent of all shots played incorporate the stun run-through. As a way of controlling the cue ball, it is by far the most useful and allows you to place the white ball in areas of the table you probably never before thought possible.

The shot itself is somewhere between the stun and the top spin – and within that range there is a variation of shots you can play to leave the white ball in different positions on the table.

The majority of stun run-through shots are played with the tip of the cue striking the white ball just above centre and just below the top. You can still use the stun run-through when hitting below centre on the white ball, but to take effect the shot must be very soft.

Below you can see the wrong way to cue for back spin. Notice the steep angle of the end of the cue to the white. Also, the bridge hand has not been lowered, there is a large gap between the cue and the cushion and the butt of the cue is raised. The bottom picture shows the correct way to cue for the back spin shot. The whole of the cue is roughly parallel to the table, the bridge hand has dropped and there is virtually no gap between the cue and the cushion.

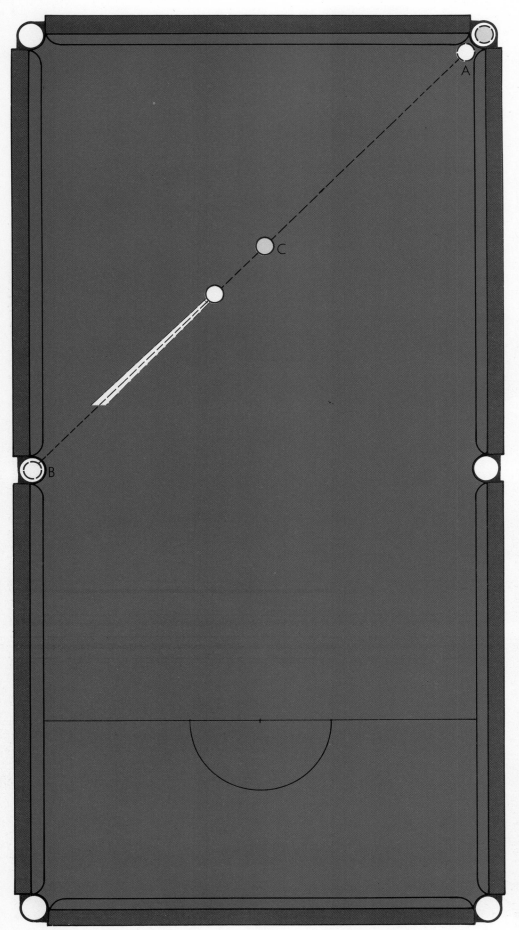

Try this exercise to get used to the effects of the main spins — top spin, back spin, stun and stun run-through. Place the pink on its spot and put the white about a foot away in a straight line between the middle and opposite corner pocket through the pink. If you put top spin on the white when potting the pink, the white (A) will travel at speed after the pink into the pocket. When playing with back spin, the white (B) will travel back in a straight line towards the centre pocket. By playing the stun shot, the white will stop on impact with the pink (position C). With stun run-through, by far the most commonly used of all spins, the white will stop somewhere between C and A, depending on how you play the shot.

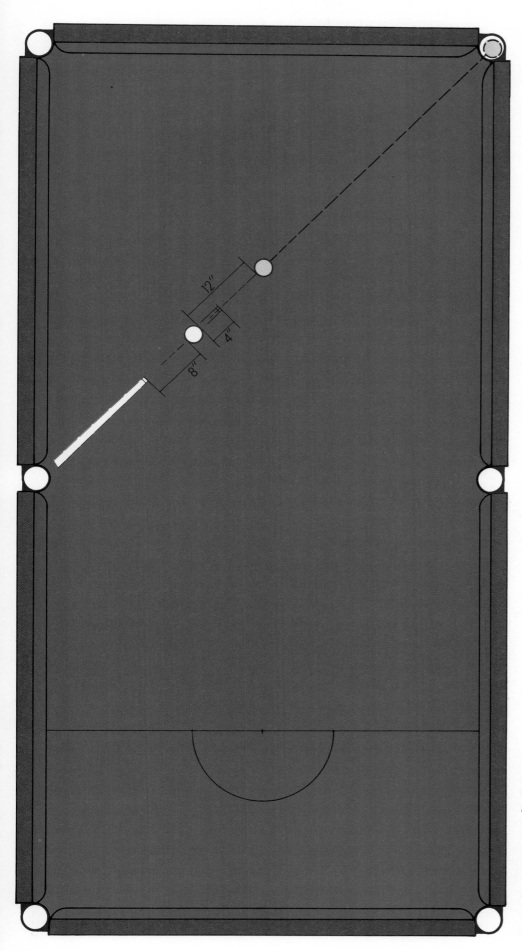

12"

4"

8"

This diagram shows the length of my back swing and follow-through when playing a stun shot in the same situation. The back swing is 8in and the follow-through 4in. Do not forget the pause when practising these exercises, which you might inadvertently do when you are concentrating on the length of the back swing.

The following three
exercises are to show the
various positions you can
achieve with the white ball
by imparting different spins
when playing the range of
potting angles at medium
pace. Although they
provide only a sample of
the positions you can reach
with the white, the exercises
are useful to help you
understand the effects of
spin and the control on the
white ball. In each case,
depending on the type of
shot you play, you can get
the white anywhere along
the cushion between points
A and C through B. You will
see from the exercises that
the thinner the contact on
the object ball, the more the
position of the white is
restricted. And the thicker
the contact, the easier it is
to impart spin.
Here you have a
threequarter-ball pot,
showing where the white
ball will hit the cushion
when played with extreme
top spin (A), stun run-
through (B) and extreme
back spin (C).

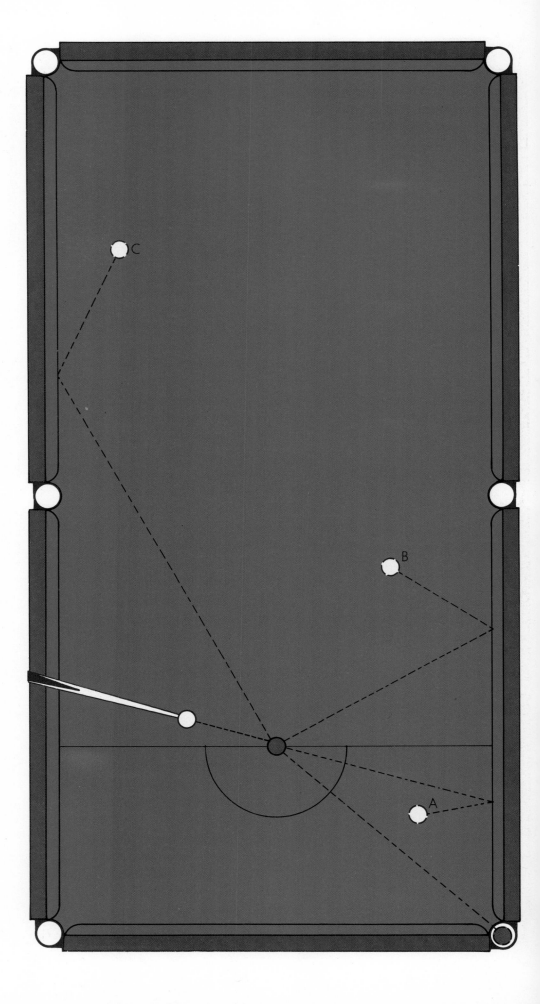

78

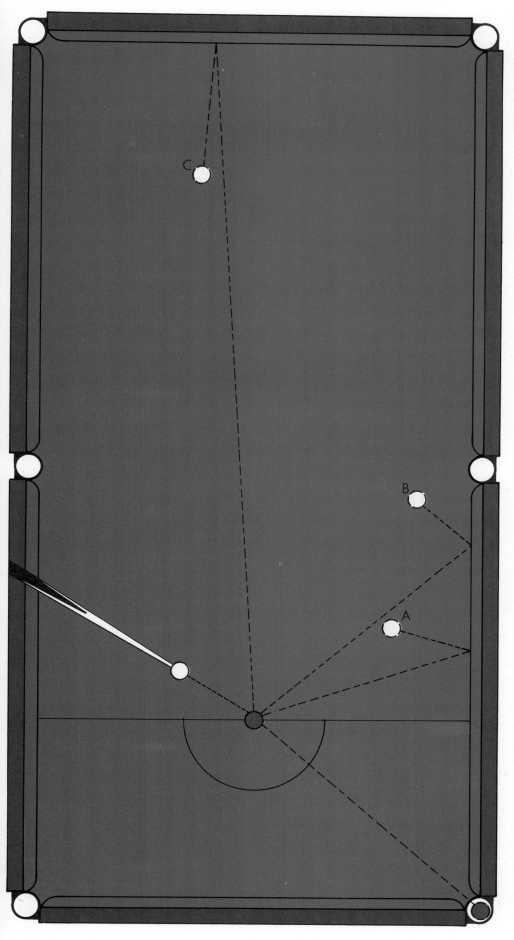

This is a half-ball pot and shows where on the cushion the white will hit when played with extreme top spin (A), stun run-through (B) and extreme back spin (C), again at medium pace.

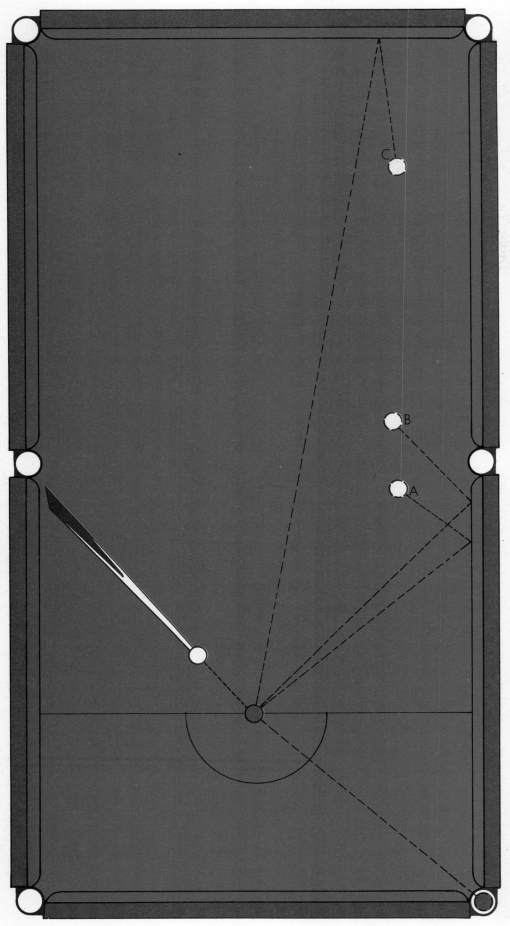

This is a quarter-ball pot and shows where on the cushion the white will hit when played with extreme top spin (A), stun run-through (B) and extreme back spin (C). You can see from this diagram how much you are restricted as far as position is concerned with a quarter-ball contact.

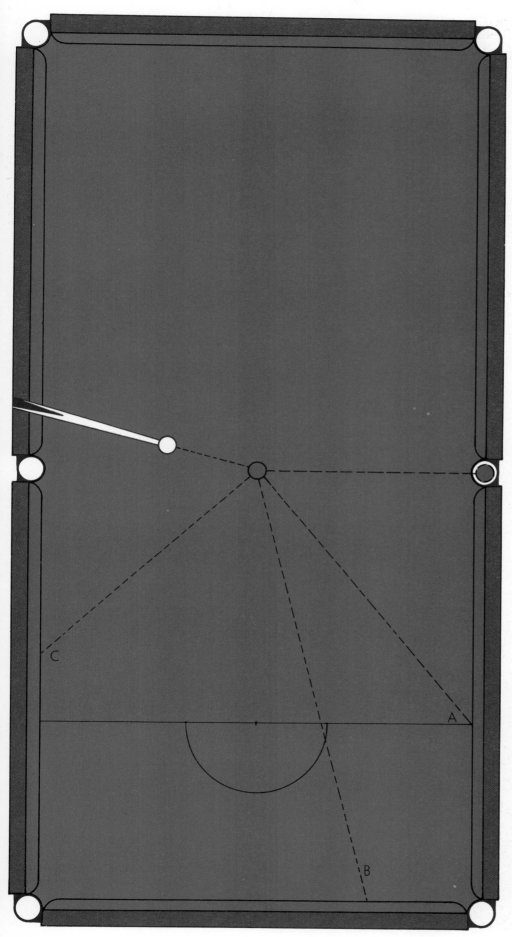

The next three exercises, which involve potting the blue on its spot, further illustrate the restrictions imposed the thinner the contact between the white and object ball gets. So you should always try to get into a position for a half or threequarter-ball contact. Here you have a threequarter-ball pot, showing where on the cushion the white will hit when played with extreme top spin (A), stun run-through (B) and extreme back spin (C).

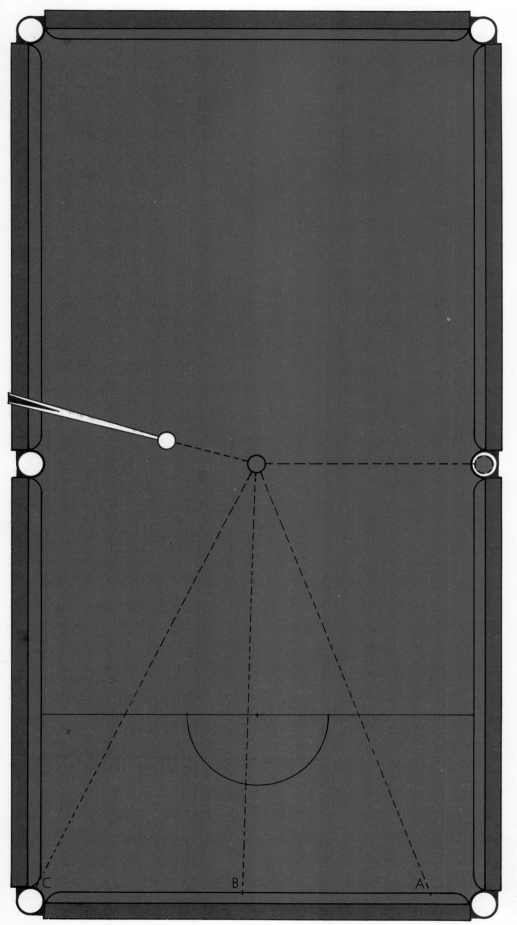

This is a half-ball pot and shows where on the cushion the white will hit when played with extreme top spin (A), stun run-through (B) and extreme back spin (C).

This shows with a quarter-ball pot where on the cushion the white will hit when played with extreme top spin (A), stun run-through (B) and extreme back spin (C). Because of the limited range of positions possible, avoid quarter-ball contact whenever possible.

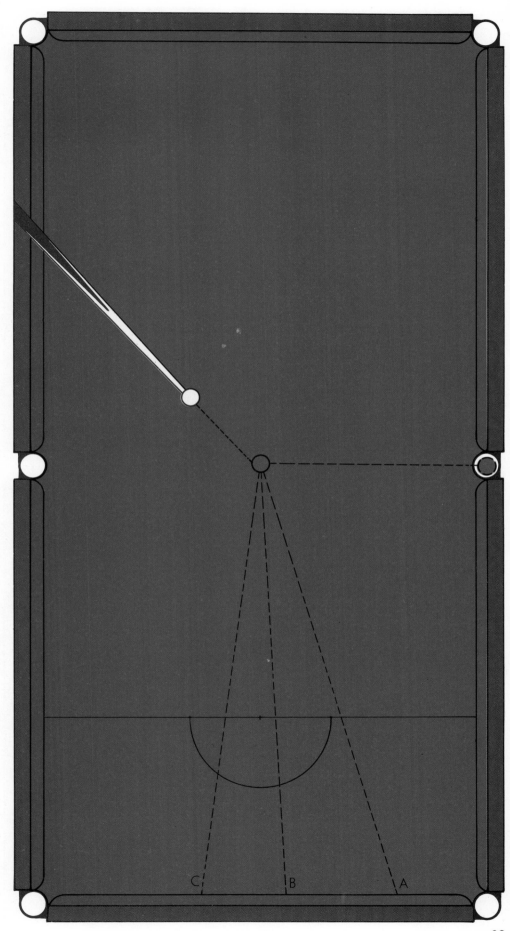

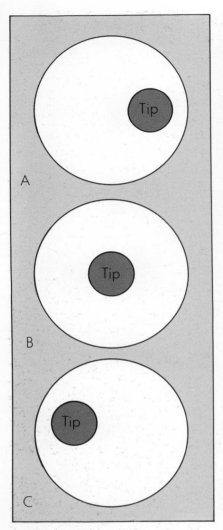

A

B

C

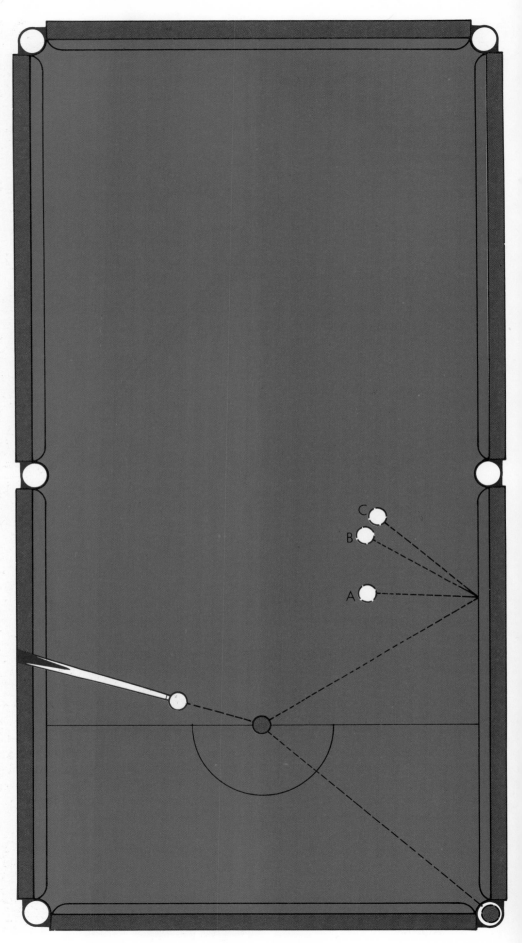

Above: Here you can see the point of contact necessary on the white ball to put on right-hand side (A), to play plain ball (B) and to put on left-hand side (C).

Right: By practising this exercise, you can check on the different effects side spin will have when playing a half-ball pot in this position. A shows the direction the white will travel in after contact with the object ball when played with right-hand side, B when played plain ball and C when played with left-hand side.

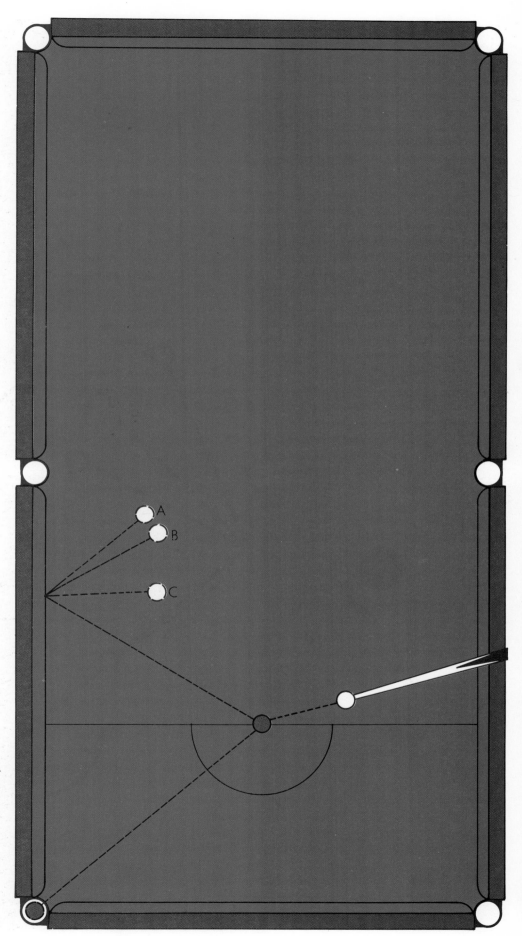

Notice that when you play this exercise from the other side of the table, the effect of the side spin is reversed. Of course, these are only examples of the possible control you can get on the white ball. By using different combinations of spin, you will naturally increase the range of positions available from each shot.

Below: This shows the point of contact necessary on the white ball to effect back spin with right-hand side (A), back spin (B) and back spin with left-hand side (C).
Right: With this exercise you can experiment on the different effects of side spin coupled with back spin on a full-ball pot. A shows the direction the white will travel in when played with back spin and right-hand side, after it has hit the cushion, B when played with just back spin and C when played with back spin and left-hand side.

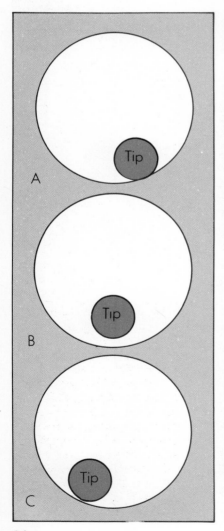

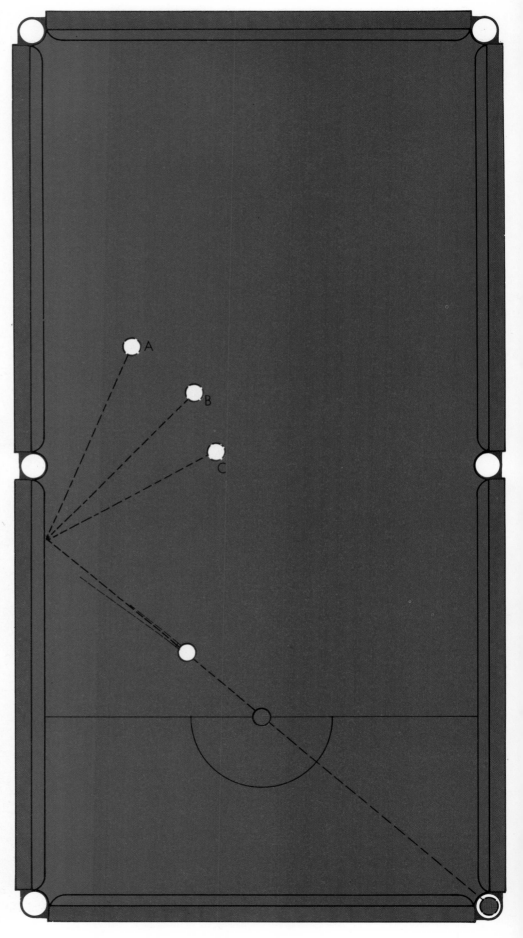

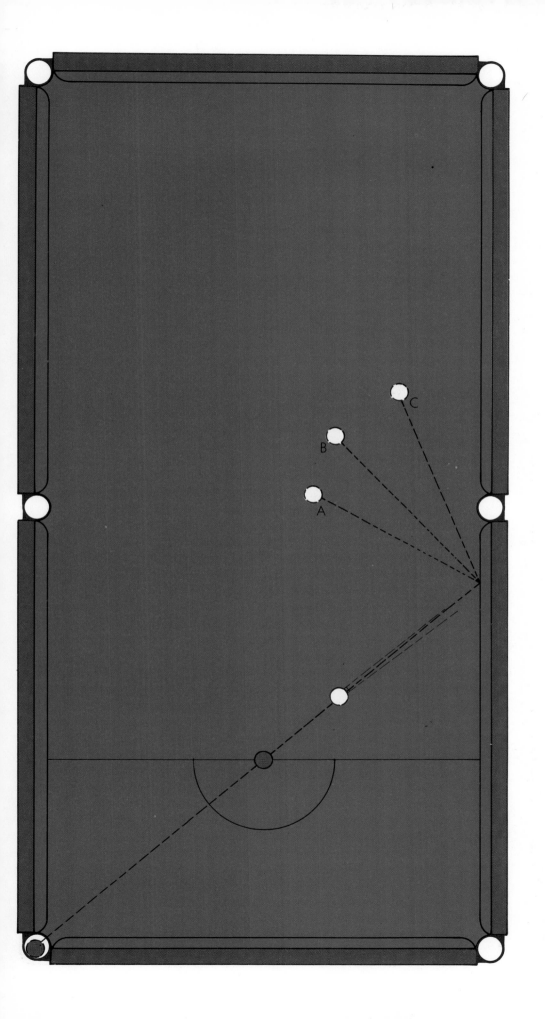

Here you can see that when you play this exercise from the other side of the table, the effect of the spin is reversed. One point you must remember when combining back spin with side is that after contact with the cushion the white will travel off in the opposite direction to the side put on the ball.

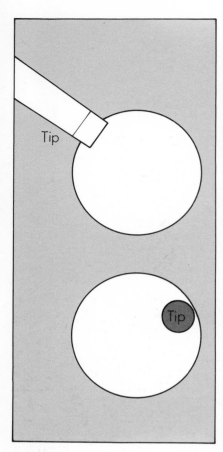

Above: The point of contact required on the white ball to effect swerve – as seen from the side view and as seen by the player.
Right: Here you can see the direction the white ball takes when played with right-hand swerve, as it goes past the left of the ball in the way and comes back on line to pot the red. To send the white the other side of the ball in the way, hit it with left-hand swerve.

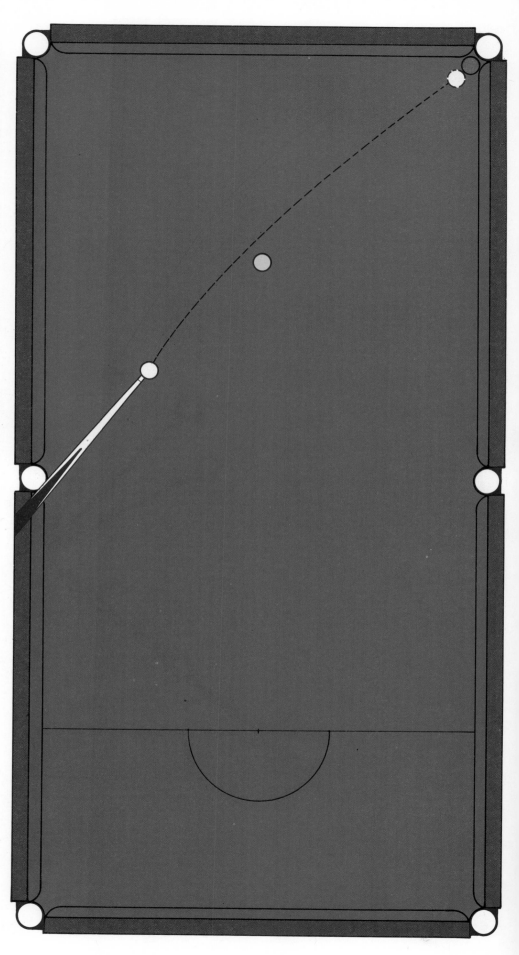

This diagram shows the maximum length of back swing and follow-through I use when playing shots of varying pace. A shows the length of each for a gentle pace shot, B for a medium pace shot and C for an extreme power shot. The follow-through is the same for medium pace and extreme power shots, illustrating that power comes totally from length of back swing and speed of cue delivery.

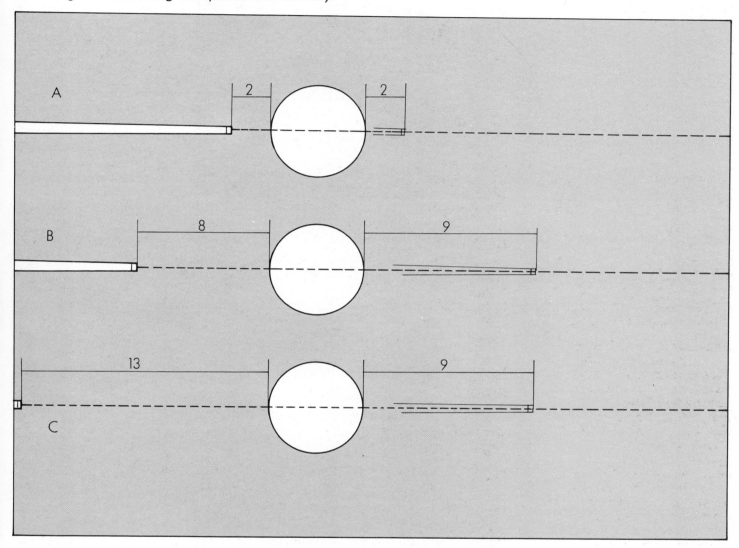

white ball, in extreme cases you may have to aim to miss the pocket by six inches in order to pot the ball. Add to this allowance in judging the potting angle the effect the nap may have on the spin as the white ball travels over the cloth and you can see how much more difficult the shot has now become.

And this goes against all I have said so far in the book — about making the game as simple as possible. With back spin and top spin, screw back and stun, you are still hitting somewhere along the centre line through the white ball — and therefore not making the shot that much more difficult. With side spin, you certainly are.

When you play the break-off shot, however, the situation is quite different. The triangle of reds is always in the same position on the table — the same distance from the white ball. Therefore you can allow for a slight discrepancy in the spin of the white, provided the cloth is in reasonable condition, and still play a respectable shot. This is a lot

different from when the balls are scattered on the table. Of course, you do not have to use side spin when you break off, but most players do.

Swerve

This shot is an exaggerated form of the side spin and would be played when you wanted to arc the white ball round other balls in the way of the object ball — for example, to get out of a snooker. It is the one time when you raise the butt of the cue deliberately and then you have to strike the extreme top side of the white with a downward motion.

As you can see, it goes against all the basic principles of technique — keeping the butt from lifting and striking the white with the cue horizontal — and is therefore a very difficult shot to control. This is why it is so rarely used even by the professionals.

If you do want to practise the shot, you will find that the width and length of the arc along which the white ball will

A full side-on view of the pause, hit and follow-through sequence when playing a power shot. Note the extra long back swing and the fact that the follow-through is the same as for a medium pace shot. And the rest of the body remains still, while only the back arm moves.

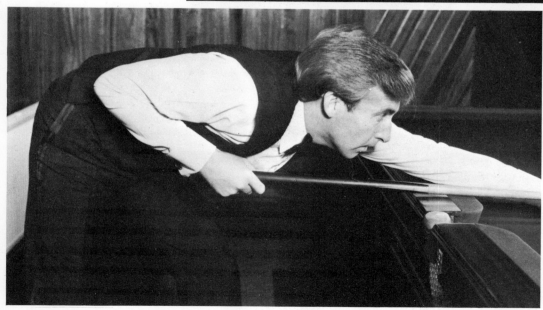

travel is determined by the pace of the shot and the amount of side you put on the white ball.

And one thing this shot will show you is what can happen if you do not hit the white correctly and accurately down the line with the cue parallel.

Using spin

Having discussed the various types of spin possible and how they work, the problem comes as to when to use them. I am afraid that you will only recognise when to use spin by practice and experience. There are so many different variations that it would be totally impractical to try to list them. You will need to set up these shots, try them out and watch what happens. Experiment with each type of spin in turn at different angles and attempt to remember what happened to the white ball.

I have found in coaching that aspiring players either have an aptitude for angles and spins or they have not. If you are one of those that have not, you will obviously have more difficulty in mastering this area of technique.

One guide to use of spin that should be of help, however, is that the thicker the contact between the white ball and the object ball, the easier it is to effect spin on impact. This means you should get the maximum effect of spin with a full-ball contact, but it will be very difficult to impart much in the way of spin with a very fine quarter-ball contact.

Power shots

The power shot does have a part to play in the game of snooker, but its use should be strictly limited since the control you need over your body, the cue and the white ball is reduced the harder you play the shot and there is a much greater chance of errors creeping in. This means that you should try to restrict its use to the simpler shots. Avoid, therefore, playing a power shot when using the rest or when putting side spin on the white.

The reason for using power is to gain a certain position on the table which cannot be reached by playing at a slower pace. It is not to see the white ball shooting round the table several times or to hear the object ball cracking into the back of the pocket.

The aim is to strike the white ball with the minimum amount of pace to achieve the maximum distance required for position on the next shot. In extreme cases, of course, this may involve using maximum power in the shot.

It is always worth bearing in mind that if you pot a red you get one point, whether it enters the pocket at 1mph or 100mph!

To put power into a shot involves a longer back swing and more pace in the cue as it comes through to strike the white ball. And, of course, this must be linked with timing. To achieve maximum power, you have to bring the tip of the cue back to the 'V' in the bridge hand. This is the furthest back you can take the cue without losing control of it. Then you must bring it through at the maximum pace possible without moving the rest of your body. In practice, of course, there is bound to be slight movement, but this must be kept to a minimum. You should still be in control of the basics — the stance, the head, the cue, etc.

To measure the maximum amount of power you can put into a shot, go back to the straight line exercise and place the white ball on the brown spot. Then hit it as hard as possible with maximum back swing and measure the number of times it travels up and down the table.

Do not get carried away with power, however. In competitions, I find that I need to use extreme power perhaps one per cent of the time. That is how little it is used. Always remember that you should only strike the ball as hard as is necessary to gain the desired position with the white ball. If you hit harder than you need, the only person to benefit will be your opponent.

Having learned to control the pace at which you play individual shots and to use the range of spins as and when they are needed, you should now be in control of the cue ball and well on the way to mastering the kind of positional play that will enable you to build up reasonable breaks, which are, of course, necessary to win frames and therefore matches.

Self-control

Chapter: 6
Self-control

Having achieved the first three controls – control of your body, control of the cue and control of the cue ball, you will have proved you have the ability. But without the fourth – and in many ways the most important – control, that of yourself, the other three are really wasted. And this control is vital at all stages of snooker, whether you are practising in the club or playing the final of a major tournament.

Basically it is about temperament (a simple word that covers so much), composure, balance and, of course, more specifically things like shot selection.

It is easy to get annoyed when something goes wrong. If you do not have self-control, the smallest things will tend to frustrate you, like missing a simple pot. But it is important to remember that, as in all sports, winning or losing can depend on just one small mistake – and, particularly, the way that mistake may affect you and your game. Whether it is a missed penalty in football or a dropped catch in cricket, the principle is the same. You must put that one slip behind you and concentrate on getting back into the game as quickly as possible. That is the ultimate proof of your character – and in the end will sort out the winner from the loser.

If you have this control and can keep your composure, you will be able to handle the many pressures that build up during a match. Without it, it is very difficult to think about the basic things in the game, such as your stance and cue action, and to concentrate on selecting the right type of shot to play. And this process of shot selection is one of the things that makes snooker such a great game – a game of decisions.

Every time you approach the table you have got to make a decision. The advantage of snooker and other still-ball games such as golf is that you have got plenty of time to make a decision. It is much harder, for example, in soccer where players have to make split-second decisions, although at least they have not got time to dwell on the decision because already something else is happening.

In snooker you have got plenty of time to make the right decision, but you need that self-control and composure to think clearly under pressure.

A talented player will have mastered the first three controls we have looked at, but it is this last control that seems to sort out the successful player from the also-ran. I have been asked so many times why certain talented players do not achieve the success their talent and ability deserves. I believe the answer lies in this control – of yourself.

One of the methods I used to help me with my self-control, particularly when undergoing the pressures of a big match. Fortunately I don't need this type of help anymore.

Before you start playing, your whole mental approach must be right. And you must always think positively. One of the hardest things for the professional is to sit out while the opponent is at the table. Although this does not affect the amateur in quite the same way, since many of the matches will be single-frame affairs, it does illustrate the problems of keeping in the right frame of mind.

When you have to sit out, it is so easy for your mind to wander. Your opponent can dominate your thoughts if you

Above: If Alex Higgins possessed greater self-control, by now he would probably be unbeatable.
Right: Steve Davis – Mr Self-control himself.

allow it and are not strong-minded enough to concentrate your attention on your own game. If you are playing well and have the right mental balance, it does not make any difference how your opponent is playing. You know that when your opportunity comes along you will be able to do the same thing.

If you have not got the right mental attitude, when your opponent is playing well you will get depressed and think that you are never going to match him. And, of course, when you get to the table, you will not.

From time to time these kind of thoughts are bound to enter your head, but the player with the right amount of self-control and the correct attitude will be able to put them out of his mind and find that bit of extra effort to think positively and play himself back into the game.

In competition, it is the easiest thing in the world to give up. We have all done it. You think to yourself: 'They've got it now so why bother to try my heart out. It's not that important if I lose.' You can always find an excuse for not trying, but there is never a reason for not doing so. Never try to cheat yourself – or the game.

It is, of course, unrealistic to expect 100 per cent performance every time you go on the snooker table, although you must start a match with that intention. You would be some sort of freak if you could do this every time. What is important is that when you know you are playing below this level you must be able to control yourself and hope that your form on the day will carry you through and that, hopefully, the next time you will be back to 100 per cent – or more.

It is, of course, impossible to reach a peak and sustain it everytime you play. So the most significant point of anyone's game is not how good is your best but how bad is your worst. You must strive to ensure that even when you are not on top form, you can still retain control over your game and maintain a reasonably consistent standard. It is far better to play just below top form consistently than to play at a peak part of the time and then badly at other times.

Ray Reardon has proved by his record that he is the type of player who is never really bad – and when he is playing well, he is very good. Steve Davis is like that too. Even when he is playing badly by his standards, he is still that much better than most other players.

The ultimate objective must be to keep control of yourself even under extreme pressure, when you are playing badly, when everything is going wrong and you just cannot pot any ball, let alone win a frame. It is easy to keep control when everything is going right and you feel on top form. It is when you feel nothing is running for you that the problem starts. In this situation, the fact is that it is not the fault of the balls or the table or bad luck, but that you have lost control and are telling yourself that you are having a bad day.

In this situation you lose control, not only of yourself but also of the other things we have talked about – the approach to the table, the stance, the cue action, the contact with the white ball and the shot selection. It is no good thinking to yourself: 'I should be winning this match. What's going wrong?' Just because you know you have the ability, this does not mean that by right you should win. If you really are good enough on the day, then you will win.

To illustrate how important this self-control is, there are times when you may get by even if one of the other controls is missing. If you have control over yourself you can often make the necessary adjustments to your game to overcome the other problems.

It is easy for people to say about a certain player that he has got a good temperament when he is winning. But it is

when he is going through a bad patch, and can pull through it relatively unscathed, that you can really say he has got the temperament.

Success breeds success and failure breeds failure. But with the truly successful man everything can breed success, even failure. That is the big difference. If you have a positive attitude and the right temperament failure today can be success tomorrow because you have sufficient control to get over the disappointment of losing. You know you have the ability to win next time.

This happened to me in the 1982/83 season. In December I beat Alex Higgins 16-15 to win the Coral UK championships and four months later, in the second round of the Embassy world championships, I lost by the odd frame to Cliff Thorburn 13-12 – and was out of the tournament.

This illustrates how thin the line is between success and failure. Whichever side of the line you happen to be on, you must be able to put that result behind you.

After the match with Thorburn people started saying: 'What went wrong?' In fact there was nothing basically wrong with my play; after all, I only lost by the odd frame. But this is a perfect example of how one frame either way can make all the difference between winning and losing. I was not playing any differently, really.

The point I want to make is that if this happens you should not panic and think you have to change some part of your game. Obviously you should check your technique all the time. But one defeat does not mean that the technique is wrong.

Matchplay
There is a world of difference between playing a friendly or practice game in the club and playing in a match – at whatever level. Even when you are trying your best against a friend, it is never the same as when you are competing in a tournament. A missed shot in a 'friendly' game may cost you the frame. If you do it in a competition, it may well cost you the match.

Suddenly that one shot becomes very important, as do all the others. Why is this? Well, it has got a lot to do with pressure and having the temperament to cope with it.

So often you will see players at the top of their form in practice before a match. Then, when they go to the table, suddenly the shots they were playing perfectly before are now going all wrong. This happens to virtually everyone at some stage or other, so you must be aware of it and face

If only Steve Davis would always keep one eye closed . . .

the reality. You may well play perfectly in practice for six days on the trot. If you can play well two nights a week in matches, you are a very lucky person.

One area where I personally think a lot of people go wrong is that before a match they practise very hard all day. They may well reach top form, pot all the balls and have large breaks. Then, when it comes to the match, they miss a fairly simple pot and they cannot believe it. They are not in the right mental state to accept the fact that on the night they may not play quite as well as in practice. The chances are that at this stage their game deteriorates even further and they go to pieces.

Of course, when you go into a match, you have to be super-confident and ultra-positive. At the same time you have got to be realistic about what could happen on the table. It is unlikely that you are going to pot everything you

Above: John Pulman's technique is still regarded as one of the best in the history of the game.
Left: Ray Reardon is one of the coolest – and therefore most deadly – players under pressure. This is the position his opponents would always like to see him in, but cannot get him there often enough.

try for, although you obviously hope you will. A lot of players, and here I include professionals, will go into a match expecting too much. Consequently, they are the ones to fall first.

So the right approach to the match is vitally important. You must want to win but at the same time you must realise that you can lose. What has helped me in my mental approach to the game is that I can accept all the things that might happen in a match so that when they do I have already thought about them and can cope with them.

If, for example, I am playing the best-of-seven frames, I realise that even against a so-called inferior player I could lose 4-0. Equally I could be 3-0 up and lose 4-3. I might even be 3-0 down against a better player and end up winning 4-3. There are many permutations and they have all happened to me during my career. I have had disastrous defeats and superb victories one after the other.

One thing in snooker you can be assured of is that everything that can go wrong or right will at some stage happen to you. If you can be ready to accept it when it comes and have the right mental approach, your match-play will benefit enormously. You can so easily go from being on top form for one shot to being rock bottom on another — and if you are not ready for it, it will hit you very hard.

Tactics

I suppose we ought to distinguish here between tactics and gamesmanship, since the two are quite different and totally separate as far as I am concerned. Now and again you will find a little gamesmanship creeping into a match, a bit of a leg-pull or the odd comment, although I rarely do it and do not believe it is that useful as a tactic.

I can only speak from experience, but I have found that when an opponent tries it on me it has always spurred me on to greater things. So gamesmanship as such has never bothered me — and I do not believe it is something you should include in your game deliberately.

Playing tactics, on the other hand, are very important in a match, but they are not a thing I would plan before a game, necessarily. People have asked me, for example, if I play slowly deliberately when I meet Alex Higgins. I think to myself: 'Well, I don't play slowly against Alex. It's just that he's so quick it makes me look slow' — although I do play slower than a lot of the professionals.

Mind you, it is easy to get carried away playing people like Alex. He can knock up a winning break in no time at all

and you are sitting there thinking: 'That would have taken me 20 minutes to do.' You can then find yourself playing quicker and getting into his pattern. So it is possible for an opponent to dictate to you mentally if you allow this to happen. This, of course, does not happen with the best players.

The way a game is played depends so much on the position of the balls on the table that you really cannot plan the type of game you play beforehand. You may find you are up against an opponent who normally plays the same type of game as yourself and then it often depends on how he plays as to what tactics you adopt — whether you play an attacking or a defensive game or a balance between the two.

Tactics will also depend on the run of the balls. Some days you will always seem to play the balls into the right positions, while at other times you can never quite get them to go where you want. I think at the end of the day it all balances out. Basically you should play the game as you find it, although for one reason or another you may make a conscious decision to play a bit tighter on a particular occasion — if, for example, you had a poor previous match.

There have been many times in my career when I have not been happy with the balance of my play. Perhaps I have gone for too many shots at the wrong time or alternatively not gone for enough shots and wondered whether the balance has been right or not.

This is one of the hardest things to judge, but there is no doubt that shot selection is a major part of tactics. Do I play this one safe or do I go for the pot? If you select the right shot at the right time then you can do more harm to your opponent than just on the scoreboard. Equally, you may decide to play four or five telling safety shots. These will not score points on the board, but they can put your opponent into all sorts of trouble.

This brings us back to making decisions and keeping the right balance. Take Steve Davis and Ray Reardon, probably the two most successful players during my career. They can both strike the perfect balance between attack and defence — when to play an attacking, albeit slightly chancey, shot and when to turn it down and play to put their opponent in trouble. They always seem to pick the right time and play the shots they want.

I believe shot selection has always been one of my strengths, especially in my amateur days when I did not have quite the same repertoire of shots I have now — or that other amateur players had at the time. I was able to win because within those restrictions I could always select the right shot at the right time.

Let us take a shot that is definitely 'on', although there is an element of risk involved. You may feel very confident of getting it, but this is where self-control comes in because it is often the hardest thing in the world to turn a shot like this down. You want to go for it and you know you are going to get it. But it takes a very good player to resist the temptation to play it. When things are not going well you always seem to make the wrong decision at the wrong time.

Of course, it does happen that you decide to go for the risky shot and get it – and, all of a sudden, the risky shot has become the right one. At other times, you go for a shot that does not appear so risky, you play it badly and it turns into a disaster. Up until then, it had looked like a shot to nothing, where if you missed it you would not leave it on for your opponent.

Where a lot of people go wrong with shot selection is leaving too much on for their opponent if they miss. This happens a lot when people try for a red, from which they will want position on a colour and have other reds open for potting afterwards. There are great risks involved here.

What I like to do – and you will see Steve Davis and Ray Reardon are the same – is, when going for a particular red, to make sure that if I miss it I only leave that red 'on'. The mistake that is often made is to leave four or five reds 'on' after the pot has been missed. If you think about it, there is not a great deal to gain from that tactic and an awful lot to lose if you do miss the shot.

To make the decision to go for that one tremendous pot means ignoring the percentages. While, of course, you may every so often get the pot, there will be many occasions when you do not – and this could be the difference between winning and losing.

But shot selection is not just about which ball to pot, should there be a choice. Or which colour to get on after potting a particular red. In many ways it is more important to know when to play safe and to recognise when a safety shot can put your opponent into trouble. Remember, a killing safety shot can win you the match.

In the professional game, most players are very confident because they are performing at a very high level. But like everyone they have their ups and downs, not just with their performances but also mentally. When you are not feeling so confident and the shots are not happening as you want, you must try to stop your opponent playing for a while, in the hope that your timing and co-ordination will come back

Alex Higgins seldom takes a rest! The style of play that has brought him the nickname of 'Hurricane' has proved popular with audiences wherever he plays.

again and, possibly, that of your opponent will drop.

I certainly believe that attack is the best form of defence, although I have myself been criticised for adopting this approach at crucial stages in matches. I remember two occasions in particular against Steve Davis. The shots I went for cost me the match, make no mistake, but I have never regretted playing them.

Never regret the shot you select. Once you have decided on the shot, you must put 100 per cent into it. Just because you do not make the shot does not mean it was the wrong shot to play in the first place. It just means you did not play it correctly. You must believe in yourself and have confidence in your ability to select the right shot at the right time. If not you will never be more than an average defensive player.

Many people would say that Ray Reardon is basically a safety player. Of course, when he plays safe he plays as safe as anyone. But if there is ever a shot on, he will go for it. When he is playing really well, he will often ignore the percentages. But he gets away with it because he is such a fine player. Like any good player, he will tighten up his game when he is playing off form, but he only plays safe when he has to.

I will always go into a match with a positive approach. Even if I take time playing the shots, I still like to play an attacking game. Sometimes I pay for it, but as long as I have attacked I can accept that. If, on the other hand, I have defended and lose, I find that is a killing blow.

Going back to those two shots against Steve Davis, the first was in the 1980 Embassy world championships when I was defending my title. From 10-3 down I came back to 10-10. I was going for the last red in the 21st frame and tried to pot it off the side cushion and then off the blue into the pocket. I missed the pot, Steve cleared the table and then went on to win the match. I still believe that one shot could have won me the match and I have no regrets about playing it.

The other occasion was in the Benson & Hedges, when I was 6-5 down to Steve in a best-of-17 match. I had been 6-3 down and was well up in the frame. I deliberately left out a red for Steve because I knew if he missed it I could go on to take the match. He potted a tremendous red, cleared the table and, instead of 6-6, I was 7-5 down. It was a calculated risk that I took – but again no regrets.

Percentage shots

Basically these are all a question of how you weigh up the percentage. Let us take an example. If there is a red 'on' in the top half of the table, you have the chance of stunning the white ball to get onto the black and hopefully go for a break.

What you have to bear in mind is that if you miss the pot on the red, you may well be leaving your opponent with a chance at three or four reds and the same black. The alternative is to go for the red pot, but bring the white ball back down for the blue. With this shot, if you miss the red you have left nothing for your opponent.

Percentage-wise, then, this is a much better shot to play. It is certainly not a defensive shot; all you are doing is cutting out the element of risk. Why leave your opponent an easy shot? Let him take the risks. If he gets them, the best of luck! But, of course, as with any other shot a percentage shot can be 100 per cent right if you get it or 100 per cent wrong if you miss it.

So, in principle, the percentage shot is where you go for the pot but aim to bring the white ball out of the danger area, usually back down towards the low colours. In the professional game the white is not necessarily safe any-where on the table. But at club level there is usually minimum risk with this type of shot.

Percentages will naturally change, depending on how well or badly your opponent is playing. If he is playing well and potting everything, then you may decide to play an attacking shot on the basis that you must get there first. Again we are back to the question of balance – and weighing up and making the right decision at the right time.

Snookers

These can be a useful part of the tactics in a game, but you must consider carefully the position of the balls on the table. At the end of the day you must decide whether you are really going to put your opponent at a disadvantage by playing for the snooker or whether you in fact end up sacrificing position yourself.

If the pack of reds is relatively intact, for example, there is not a lot of point in attempting a snooker from the bottom of the table since your opponent should have little difficulty in hitting the reds. It can, of course, be of great value when there are three or four reds at the top and the white is at the bottom, in which situation your opponent may very well leave the reds on in attempting to play the snooker.

There is no doubt it can be a winning shot, but everyone I think would rather prefer to pot a long red and clear the table to win than win from snookering the opponent.

It is part of the ammunition of the game, however, and many matches at all levels have been won and lost with the snooker.

Working at
your game

Chapter: 7
Working at your game

Being realistic, I know that I am not going to win every tournament I play in. What I do is to aim to keep as high a percentage of wins as possible. If I regularly get through to quarter-finals, semi-finals and finals, I know I am winning more matches than I am losing. Of course you must always have belief in your ability and work hard in every competition – in every game, when it comes to it. But basically your aim should be to win more times than you lose.

The 1982/3 season was my worst since turning professional. Although I won two major tournaments, my percentage of matches won was the lowest in five years. I put this down to two things really: I was trying to alter my technique, which was the main reason; but I also felt I was stale through too much practice. You have to be in love with the game all the time you are playing and, for a while, I lost this feeling due mostly to the fact that I was spending too much time practising.

I do not see any point in practising for six to eight hours a day, since I cannot concentrate for that length of time. When I try to do it, I start making sloppy mistakes and the exercise becomes a waste of time. I think it is important for every player to realise when this is happening and, if necessary, put down the cue and stop playing for a while.

There are times in practice when I am on top form and can clear the table time and again. Then I see no point in carrying on, so I put the cue back in its case. Even when I am not playing that well, if I cannot make any progress I would stop and go back to it later. And the one point you must never lose sight of is that snooker is not about hitting balls around the table all day long in practice. It is about playing and winning matches – and making sure you are in the right frame of mind every time you compete.

Obviously, however, you will have to spend a lot more time than normal on practising different techniques – and this was the situation I was in. Apart from altering my bridge, I had until 1980 done nothing with my technique. Strangely I had played all my amateur snooker with a low bridge hand, fingers together and flat on the table. But obviously it was restricting me from playing certain shots and in 1977 I decided to raise the hand and spread the fingers to enable me to get more grip on the table and a firmer bridge. Until then I never really understood why I always hit the bottom of the white ball, although many people had pointed this out to me.

It was not until 1980 that I decided to look at my technique and try out some alterations. I had always had what I call a slight pumping action in my cue. What happens with this is that the cue is going down as it hits the white ball and the follow-through is also on the way down. This was where my timing and co-ordination came in.

Then I watched Steve Davis, who looked so good on the shot that I thought I would try out aspects of his technique. So I started levelling out the cue action, so that when I feathered the cue kept more parallel to the table. I also brought my chin down onto the cue. This of course altered the height of projection of the cue.

At about this time the cloths on tournament tables changed; they got thinner. This affected my style of play, because I have always enjoyed touch play – hitting the ball slowly and getting it to stop in a certain position. I found I had to change the shot to get the same effect and suddenly my normal pattern of positional shots was not working as before.

That season – 1980/1 – was a very successful one for me, since I was reaching the semi-final or final stage of most of the tournaments and possibly, if Steve Davis had not been in such phenomenal form, would have won more tournaments. So I felt that the change in my cue action and style of touch play had proved to work and that I had made the right decision.

By the end of the following season I had decided that possibly there were other parts of my technique that I should look at. I was beginning to understand a lot more about the mechanics of snooker action because at this time I had agreed a contract with the Mackworth group of clubs in South Wales to spend time coaching. The experience gave me a much greater insight into technique since now I was having to explain it to other people.

Having altered my bridge and more recently straightened and levelled off my cue action, I now decided to try out a different timing with the new cue action by altering my feathering. At the same time I thought I would experiment with the co-ordination of my eyes to the cue action, since this is connected to the timing of the shot as well.

Where the eyes finally focus when the shot is played varies from player to player. Some watch the white ball, some the object ball. I have always flicked my eyes from one to the other. This is, if you like, my built-in timing mechanism.

So I tried to slow down my feathering, which in effect meant slowing down the speed of the cue coming back and forth. I also practised lengthening the feathers. When I reached the pause position on the final back swing, I tried

Even Steve Davis has made a few minor alterations to his technique since he took the snooker world by storm.

to focus my eyes on the object ball. This I found very difficult to do. Instinctively my eyes were drawn to the white ball. To give you an example of what I mean, it is rather like watching your favourite programme on television when somebody comes into the room to talk to you. You turn your attention to them, but all the time you are drawn back to the television.

But I persevered and found that it did help me with certain shots, such as half-ball and angled cuts. I found it easier when I kept my eyes on the line – or direction – of the shot more than the object ball going into the pocket.

I also decided to try and cut timing down in my action – at the pause stage – so that if I was not timing the ball that well there would be less chance of error and, hopefully, I could still maintain a reasonable standard. In fact, with my new cue action – slower feathers and longer back swing – I was tending to pause longer as well. In lengthening the cue action and timing here, I was slowing down the speed of delivery of the cue as well. So I had to get a balance between a longer backswing and a shorter pause.

What I was attempting to do was virtually to rebuild my cue action, which amounted to a major change in my technique. It was almost like going out onto a familiar stretch of road to find that all the speed limits had been changed round, diversions introduced and new sets of traffic lights put into operation. What before I had done instinctively, suddenly I had to start thinking about from scratch.

Most people advised me not to mess about with a well-established cue action. But having made some changes, just because I had a few bad results I did not stop using the new parts of my technique. I was not concerned about my immediate performances as much as how I would be playing over the next 10 to 15 years and more.

After a while I found these alterations to my technique were working quite well in practice and at times I seemed to be timing the ball perfectly. I thought that perhaps there was something there, although at the back of my mind I kept thinking about the success my original technique had brought me over the years. The real test, however, was to

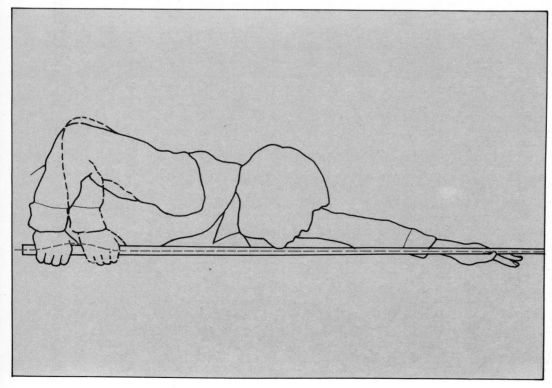

This shows my original pumping action, which I have since straightened out slightly. It was caused by the extreme length of back swing coupled with the fact that I was not opening out my grip as the cue went further back. Although this action will never look correct technically, you can see how my cue did straighten out. Just before I hit the white ball, it would be in a horizontal position.

come when I tried the new technique out in competition.

What I found when I started using it in tournaments was that subconsciously some of the old technique was drifting back into my new game and preventing me from putting all the things I had worked on into practice. In a way, it is like driving a very fast car for the first time. You want to see how fast it will go but something inside holds you back. Because you are not quite sure what will happen and whether or not you can control it, you will take it stage by stage, although you really want to put your foot down and go the whole way.

This was the problem I faced in tournaments. I did not play very well because I was indecisive in my approach. To give yourself any chance in a match, you must be 100 per cent mentally tuned up to play. I found myself torn between two styles – and so, naturally, my game suffered. I remember meeting Clive Everton in the first round of the Welsh championships, having decided to put all of my new technique into practice. Although I won 6-1, I knew I had not performed that well. I think 6-4 would have been a fairer reflection of the play. I then had to play Ray Reardon and made up my mind I was going to stick with it, even if I did not pot a ball. I started off well and went 2-1 up, Ray then levelled the score with a 50 clearance and my game just collapsed. I was hitting right across the ball and my whole timing mechanism had been thrown out.

One thing this taught me was that you cannot expect to test new techniques against one of the best players in the world first time and expect to come out winning. But the experience was a valuable one and I was pleased I had tried it. I think it must be a similar experience to taking a new horse round the jumps at Wembley. You know with your original horse you can go clear without any problem. With the new one, you must expect to knock down the odd jump or two but there has to be a first time for everything.

Going back to snooker, possibly if I had stuck with the new technique and tried it out for a longer period I could have perfected it. But I hate not playing well and this persuaded me to go back to my original technique.

The lesson to be learned in all this is that you should experiment every so often to see whether there are ways in which you can improve your game. It can cost you a match

One aspect of the game I have been working at particularly hard – keeping Steve Davis in his seat!

or two in the process, but at the end of the day you may well find that certain aspects actually help you.

Equally, I feel strongly that you should have alternatives available when things are not going well. Perhaps your timing starts to let you down or you lose some of the co-ordination. If you have practised other ways, you can always introduce them into the game at any stage to see whether they make any difference.

But, as I have already pointed out, there is a world of difference between practice and matchplay. The things you have practised for hours and done so well suddenly do not work in the match.

In a way, it is like taking a driving test. You are controlling the car perfectly in lessons and doing all the right things prior to the test. You then get into the car with the examiner and suddenly everything seems to have changed. The clutch has moved, the car has got wider, the gears do not seem as smooth. It is, of course, the same car, but the pressures that have built up make it all seem so different.

And this is what happens in a match. You must bear this in mind if you decide to change your technique at this stage. Do not expect your game to be as smooth and controlled as before. But that is not to say that you should not try new techniques. See what happens over a period before you decide to drop them. They may well help your game in the long run.

Practice

One of the questions I am always being asked is: 'How many hours a day do you practise?' There is no answer to this, since it varies on the individual, his commitments and many other considerations. But practice is, of course, an essential part of learning any game. You will only ever master all the techniques I have talked about by working at them, practising them over and over again – and even then, you are not guaranteed success.

But I regard it as equally important that practice should always have a positive effect. Just because someone tells you to practise four hours every day, this does not mean

Steve Davis is one of the most fanatical players about practice in the modern game.

you should follow the advice slavishly. If you feel, for whatever reason, you are not gaining any benefit from lengthy practice, it is far better to put down your cue and walk away from the table. Go back later, pick up the cue and try again.

My attitude to practice would never meet with universal approval, but it works for me and, as with the instruction and advice throughout the book, may suit your personality and temperament. This is not to suggest that you can happily ignore practising. Whether you like it or not, without it you will never reach a reasonable standard – let alone that of a top professional. But you must approach it intelligently and work out a programme or discipline that suits you.

When I played as a schoolboy, like many people of my age I wanted to get to a table every spare minute of the day possible. Courting and then marriage obviously got in the way and took me away from my practice. I still played a lot – at least an hour every day – but much less than I used to. It was not until 1971 when, as a postman, I had seven weeks off work due to the Postal Strike that I really got back into the game. I played solidly every day and came on in leaps and bounds. This gave me the confidence to decide to enter some national tournaments. I entered the Welsh amateur championships and was runner-up in my first year. This was the first time I realised I could compete against better players.

Believe it or not, I felt my career really took off after I had suffered two hammerings – 4-0 each time – at the hands of John Prosser and Elwyn Richards, both top Welsh amateurs. In both cases I realised that there was nothing they were doing that I could not do on the table if I was playing well, which gave me the extra boost I needed.

By this time we had a family and I was playing a lot more competitive snooker, although I had less and less time to practise. From this I realised – and still believe – that one competitive match of any type is worth a week's practice. By now I was competing at the highest level in the amateur game, but still only putting in on average an hour a day.

When I look at some of today's professionals, they seem to practise all day, every day. I find this impossible to do. Admittedly, when I gave up work and turned professional in 1978, I started practising four or five hours a day. Although until then I had never bothered to find out, I began to think that there must be room for improvement in my game. I had had my share of success and failure, but until then had never put in any hard practice to work at the weaker parts of my game.

So having done much of the groundwork as a youngster, I was now going through a crash course to see what parts of my game needed improving and making sure they did. Despite this, I would regard myself as a lazy professional, unlike players such as Steve Davis and Doug Mountjoy who will practise for hours every day when they can. Tony Meo, on the other hand, does not like to practise that much; nor, I suspect, does Ray Reardon who will put in spells but is generally of the same attitude as myself.

The point I am trying to make about practice is that you have to go through the initial stage of learning the basic techniques. This will involve playing as much as you can as regularly as you can – as long as you are enjoying it. The next stage is trying to improve and develop your game – and here perhaps practice does not have to be quite so rigid. I find I can now divide this up into the practice I do for the enjoyment of playing snooker and the practice I do for work.

For me now, hard practice would be a week's work on the table before a big tournament. By many people's standards, this is nothing. But it is what suits me and this is what you must aim to do – work out what is best for you. You must strike that balance which enables you to get in the right frame of mind for a match but not to go stale by the time you get to the table.

This can happen. I may be playing exceptionally well in practice when there is no pressure. In the match, however, suddenly I am missing those shots that came so easily before and it seems as though the whole world has collapsed. Equally it can go the other way. I may not have put in as much practice as I would have liked and, when the match arrives, I tell myself this and decide I must try that much harder. Because I am not expecting to play that well, I do not get that disappointed when something goes wrong. So I am able to keep my self-control and feel more composed.

I am not suggesting from this that you should go into a match unprepared. Equally you should not overdo the preparation. Somewhere there must be a balance between the two.

One very important point about practice is that you should also use it to maintain your performance. You are not going to increase your overall skills, necessarily, but you must use it to maintain the standard of play you have reached. So never think that because you feel you are playing well you don't have to practise. You do – and must.

*If prizes were ever awarded for practice and hard work,
then Doug Mountjoy would always be winning them.*

My top players

Chapter: 8

My top players

Without doubt, Steve Davis is the best player I have ever played against. You only have to look at the facts. Nobody else has won as many major competitions in such a short space of time.

But you have to appreciate how much the game has changed in recent years and realise that discussion on who is the best player of all time is really meaningless. In their hey-day, both Joe Davis and Ray Reardon were great players. But in each case, when they were at their peak, conditions were very different.

As I mentioned earlier, over the years there have been major developments in snooker. The quality of the tables and balls has improved enormously; the pockets have got 'bigger'. The opposition has improved. And today there are many more competitions and tournaments and therefore much more pressure on the players. Technically, too, the game has made great strides.

I have only seen Joe Davis on film and, therefore, it would be unfair to make a judgement as to whether he was better than Steve Davis. Of course, Joe was a legend in his own lifetime – and there are not many of those in any sport. His record speaks for itself, since he was undisputed champion for 20 years. Admittedly there was not the same opposition about at the time, but you must bear in mind that Joe had to be an innovator. He had no one to mould himself on, no one to copy. He had to invent the shots and originate the techniques.

To my mind, Steve Davis is technically the best player the game has ever seen. I do not think Joe's technique quite matches it, but then Joe had many other assets that helped make him the great player he was.

But the key to success – even greatness – is not so much about winning. More important than this is the way you win. The significant point about Steve's successes is how often he wins frames at the first attempt. It is one thing to check the scoresheet and look at the number of large breaks a particular player had. But hidden behind these statistics, it may be that both players missed shots in between and the eventual winner had to pay a number of visits to the table to secure his frame-winning break. Where Steve can be so devastating is that he can kill a frame stone dead on his first real opening in the game. And even when he does not manage that, usually his second or third visit is decisive. That requires the highest standard of play and it is one of the reasons why Steve is – and has proved to be – such a great player. Mind you, I know so much more about him and his game since I have played him so many times and

have therefore got a better look at him than at any other player at their peak.

Unfortunately I never played Ray Reardon during his golden years in the mid-1970s. I was, of course, an amateur player then, but Ray was always my hero. I have had a great deal of enjoyment watching him play and have probably learned more from him than from any other player. During those winning championship years, he was virtually unbeatable. If he lost any match, it was a sensation. But, of course, at that time there were very few people who could beat him. He knew that and mentally this helped his approach to each match.

One sign of a great player is the way in which he can fight his way back to the top, which is something Ray had to do after a lean spell of two-and-a-half years following the Embassy world championships in 1978. During this time he never won a major tournament, but he did signal his return to the top grade when he was runner-up to Alex Higgins in the Embassy world championship in 1982 and followed this

Left: Steve Davis – the very best, even if he couldn't afford to have a haircut!
Below: Ray Reardon dominated the game in the Seventies.

Left: Alex Higgins always generates a special atmosphere when he comes into the hall.
Below left: John Spencer is one of the most polished professionals in the game.
Below: One of my few regrets in snooker is never to have played Joe Davis — nor to have seen him play live.

John Pulman always looked as though he had been born with a cue in his hand.

with appearances in both the professional and pro-am Pontin finals, which involves a very hard week of snooker. Previously that year he had won the Yamaha and the Professional Players Tournament and was starting to play a lot better again. His comeback, against the toughest of opposition, gave hope to a lot of people in the game who had gone through similar experiences.

The pressures in the game have definitely increased, particularly so since matches are now played over far fewer frames than, for example, in Joe Davis's time. When you were playing the best of 145 frames over two weeks (as Joe did against Horace Lindrum in 1946), the best man had to win. There was not the pressure there now is of knowing that if you drop three or four frames you can be out of the match. And with this in mind, your whole mental attitude has to be different.

Whether Joe Davis would have adapted his game successfully to modern conditions, no one can say. All you can say is that, during the dark days of snooker, his impact was tremendous and there is no questioning the fact that he was the best around.

Steve Davis must rate as the most complete player. There is really nothing lacking in his game; he is as strong in one department as another. If Ray Reardon has a weakness, then it is probably in his power; he has never been a powerful player. But in other respects, these two are quite similar. They have the perfect balance – knowing exactly when to attack and when to defend – and are very strong

on potting.

Of the other players, you have to acknowledge the fact that John Pulman won eight world championships, although he would admit himself that he was not in the same class as Joe Davis.

Then there is Fred Davis, who collected eight world titles and really took over the limelight after his brother Joe. John Spencer won the world championships three times and was rated by some as the best cueist ever seen.

On his day, Alex Higgins is a tremendous player. He is, of course, very erratic; but that is what makes him so exciting to watch. You have only to look at the audiences he attracts everywhere he plays to realise that he has got a certain charisma about him. He always generates a special atmosphere when he comes into the hall. I have always had a great deal of respect for his game.

For reasons already stated, I find it impossible to separate my top players into any order. Trying to make comparisons between Joe Davis, Ray Reardon and Steve Davis would be an insult to them and an unfair reflection on their individual abilities and talents. But there is no doubt in my mind that these are the three 'greats' of snooker and between them they have done more to project the game to its current dizzy heights than any other players in the history of the sport.

The future

Chapter: 9
The future

The opportunities that have opened up in snooker over the last few years are enormous, when I think back to the time I turned professional – in 1978. Then there were only two professional tournaments in which you could hope for a break-through to the 'big-time' – the Coral UK and the Embassy world championships. These were the only open tournaments; all the others – another three or four – were invitation only.

Today the picture is very different. There has been a remarkable increase in the prize money available, too. When I won the world title in 1979, it was in the region of £35,000. In just five years it has soared to around £200,000. And in the 14 major tournaments of the 1983/4 season, total prize money is nearly £1 million.

If you can break into the top professional game today, the picture has changed dramatically. And one aspect that has done as much as anything to bring this about is television. The growth in snooker coverage, popularised with the ever-increasing number of colour televisions, has brought the game into millions of homes that had never seen it before. This has enabled youngsters to see how the game is played professionally, watch the techniques used and learn from the best.

In the past very few people had the opportunity of watching the top players. When they did, it was a big event that happened all too rarely. And as a player, you hoped through local tournaments to meet one or two better players so that you could test your ability and hopefully improve your standards. But it was a long, gradual process. Whereas then you would probably be in your 30s or 40s before you reached a high enough standard to play the game professionally, now there are many more much younger players with this ability. They are able to play a lot more snooker in a much shorter space of time so that they are able to achieve what, as a working man, it would have taken 10 years before.

The facilities have grown and improved through the years as well. Now clubs are opening up all over the country, enabling more and more people to take up the game and play regularly – and the conditions of play are unrecognisable compared to those I used to play in when I was a boy.

Hand-in-hand with the increase in television coverage has come sponsorship, an inevitable by-product that has injected so much money into the sport. Snooker in general – and professional players in particular – owe much to the support from major companies over the last few years, which has transformed the game and its opportunities.

If you go back to 1978 and before, there was little snooker coverage on television. The first, major break-through came with the screening, albeit limited, of the world championship. Naturally the other major tournaments followed. There was, of course, *Pot Black* which from its early days proved enormously popular with viewing audiences. However, I have never felt that the one-frame matches really got across to the public what the game of snooker was all about.

The game came to life, I feel, with the world championships, when viewers could follow the ups and downs of the top players, the suffering when they lost and the jubilation when they won. It created a marvellous atmosphere which until then had been missing.

Growth of the game

With the growth in clubs and the ever-increasing enthusiasm of young people for the game – competitive and otherwise – the future definitely looks bright. Children may simply start by watching it played on television, possibly knocking the balls around on a small-size table in the back room, but then the game really gets to them. They join clubs, play in the local leagues and from there, who knows?

I do believe that we have probably reached the stage where there is enough snooker on television – and I personally doubt that there will be more tournaments screened and more hours of coverage. But who is to say, since viewing figures are still remarkably encouraging.

Certainly from the playing and trade point of view, there seems no end to the boom that has made snooker one of the most popular sports in the country.

Women and snooker

I have always been a great watcher of the game – at all levels – and, equally, enjoy coaching. Over the last year or two I have watched a fair amount of women's snooker and, in fact, have coached Sian Newbury, who is one of the top players. Although at present the standard is a lot lower than that of the men, I have noticed a definite improvement.

Of course, you will not see a dramatic change overnight. It takes years for the standards to grow in any new game – new, that is, to the people playing it. As in any other sport, they play to their own standards and they compete hard against each other – and that is what the competitive spirit is all about.

The bright lights . . .

Sian Newbury – Pontin Ladies champion in September 1983 and one of the top lady players in the game.

At present you will not see the women make 50 breaks to win frames, but that does not mean they are not trying. They try very hard, in some cases harder than the men because of the limitations of their game. They may not have the same range of shots, particularly when it comes to power, and have more difficulty of shot selection, therefore. But I am sure this side of snooker will make progress. Already a group of top women players has been formed – Ladies Snooker International – which is involved in challenge matches, exhibition and promotion work.

It would be a great thing for snooker if the women's game developed further and more and more could compete on a major scale. After all, about 60 per cent of the television audience for snooker are women – and to think there was a time when you could not find a single one watching the game.

The great thing now is that the new clubs are open to the whole family. This means women and children can go along to watch – and to play if they want. This is making snooker much more of a family entertainment, which is definitely an encouraging sign for the future of the sport.

In the past, playing snooker in the club for hours on end was generally frowned upon and the real enthusiasts were accused of having had a mis-spent youth. I believe that has to a great extent been changed with the progress that has been made within the game at all levels. Parents can now be proud to acknowledge their children as potential snooker players.